Sarah Pratt McLean Greene

**Stuart and Bamboo**

A Novel

Sarah Pratt McLean Greene

**Stuart and Bamboo**
*A Novel*

ISBN/EAN: 9783337026837

Printed in Europe, USA, Canada, Australia, Japan

Cover: Foto ©Thomas Meinert / pixelio.de

More available books at **www.hansebooks.com**

# STUART AND BAMBOO

## A Novel

BY

### SARAH P. McLEAN GREENE

AUTHOR OF

"VESTY OF THE BASINS" "CAPE COD FOLKS" ETC.

NEW YORK AND LONDON

HARPER & BROTHERS PUBLISHERS

1897

## By SARAH P. McL. GREENE.

**VESTY OF THE BASINS.** A Novel. Post 8vo, Cloth, $1 25.

One of the sweetest, freshest of novels. . . . There are scenes of humor and of pathos.—*Philadelphia Bulletin.*

It is a work of real genius—strong, true, brave, and tender. It is a story to be read and remembered.—*Newark Advertiser.*

A story of the far "down east" coast of Maine, wonderfully realistic in its portrayal of life and manners among the people of a remote fishing-village, and rich in episodic incidents, amusing, sentimental, and dramatic.

### NEW YORK AND LONDON:
### HARPER & BROTHERS, PUBLISHERS.

# STUART AND BAMBOO

## CHAPTER I

"Second class to Yarmouth," said Margaret.

The man, giving quick automatic glances in the rush of business, laid down a first-class ticket.

"I said 'second class.'"

"Pardon," said the man, complying—and might be pardoned, for Margaret Stuart stood there plainly and egregiously "first class."

"Carriage, lady?" "Porter, lady?"

Margaret walked on, unheeding, with her burdens.

She found a place in the crowded car at last, but tête-à-tête with a bounteous moth-

1

er and her surrounding galaxy of soiled
cherubs.

"Widow?" said this woman at length,
kindly.

"Yes."

"Childern?"

"Yes—in heaven," Margaret added, low,
for she had been a Sunday-school teacher
in the First —— Church at D——.

"I surmised it from the heft o' your
weeds; they was babies, I opine—ye ain't
over twenty-five."

"I am thirty."

"Sho! Well, well—so be—they're better
off with God."

"Do you not think God is with them
here?" said Margaret, so fine a quality of
sarcasm in her sweet low voice the woman
looked safely incredulous.

"It's a thought, anyway!" she admitted,
guardedly, and proceeded to open her lunch-
basket.

Margaret was now the only one in the
car who was not eating. Freight-bound for
the night with the rest, she appeared to be

without resource for refreshment. The matron looked over her disordered food, imprinted everywhere with babies' fingers—the milk-bottles were out of the question. But a trim little country milliner, the other side of the aisle, took her life in her hand and solved the problem.

"Try one of my sponge-cakes, madam," said she, offering it to Margaret on a napkin. "I made 'em myself. Do! I'll feel real hurt if you despise it."

"Despise it!" said Margaret, thanking her as she took the gift, and they saw, now that her still face broke into a smile, a possibility of humor not to be excelled, even in a second-class carriage, mingled with a haunting sort of loveliness.

"I'll bet," said a buxom professional nurse, who was engaged in a flirtation with a blacksmith, as noisy and pronounced as the play of the latter's own anvils—"I'll bet, now, that lady yonder 's travellin' off on her temper. I know style. I've nursed 'em. Yes, sir! she's got her sails set for a cruise in the schooner *Holy Spunk!*" She marched over to Margaret with a piece of bread in her wholesome hand and dropped it in her lap. "Eat that before you eat your cake," said she; "it's better for ye."

So! Not only to be fed as by ravens, but on hygienic principles!

"Try one o' my home-made pickles for a ralish," said another voice. A cucumber as large as a small kitten was deposited by the side of the bread.

The milliner had plenty of sponge-cakes, the nurse had superfluous bread, the pickle-woman had profuse specimens of the same abnormal development; but a youthful pair on the front seat had just one orange between them wherewith to moisten their biscuits.

After a whispered conversation the boy arose, walked solemnly to Margaret, lifted his hat, as his girl had strictly enjoined upon him to do, and without a word placed the orange in the general contribution-box —her lap.

Margaret, meditating many things, waited a little before she went over to the donors.

"I have eaten so much—people have been so kind—I really cannot take this," she said, with a manner that satisfied them; and the youth, who was a carpenter, now divided the fruit with his girl as mathematically as if he were working with chisel and plane.

A laugh startled Margaret as she turned and stood face to face with a young woman, only the back of whose restless auburn head had been visible to her before.

She sat among a cluster of admirers of the most overgrown sylvan type, whose verdancy she evidently appreciated, for her head was at once thrown back with a contemptuous indifference to all things, waiting for the charity-fed lady to pass on.

She herself, with her radiant brown eyes and hair, was a Hebe in form, with features suggestive of a Madonna; long lashes — in this moment of social abeyance — drooping, dove-like, on her cheeks.

"What a beauty!" thought Margaret, passing on to her seat.

As she did so Hebe, with insolent precipitancy, became again an informing sun in

the midst of her satellites. Pleasantry so
cheerful as to partake even of resounding
cuffs and slaps reached Margaret's ears;
presently she saw the auburn head crowned
with a male hat, ungallantly forced there
by the largest bumpkin of all, who had assumed Hebe's own. His fat weak face, thus
adorned, took on a simpering look, and the
poor straggling feathers, so jaunty on their
owner, drooped strangely over his asinine
ears.

From this marked nucleus of wit the
mirth became general: the matron opposite
Margaret shook with unimbittered laughter.
"I'm goin' to give that hawk of a girl something to do!" said she. She took up the
smallest squirming baby and went over to
Hebe. "Would you hold him a little for me,
miss?" she said, with the simplest natural
confidence; "he's tired o' me; they like a
change o' arms."

Hebe was under the reckless and resentful
consciousness that she was tabooed, even in
a second-class caravan, for her wild conduct; a quick eager light came over her

face as she reached out her arms for the child.

"Quit, now!" said she, authoritatively, to the renewed bantering of her admirers, and henceforth deigned no rejoinder to them as she tossed the delighted baby in her buoyant young arms.

The rejected rose in a body and shuffled, grinning foolishly, out to the smoking-car.

The baby, with growing jubilance, at last thrust its ecstatic fingers into Hebe's hair; she twisted about to extricate the little fist and her eyes met Margaret's; she gave the older woman a glance, half of triumph, half with a long, unmistakable gleam of dislike and defiance in it.

"I can smell gov'ment bonds, fam'ly trees, and indigo - blue Presbyterians clear the whole length of this car," said she to the child's mother, who came to her assistance. "Why don't she travel with her own set?"

"She answers all my questions polite enough," returned the matron; "but, after all, I don't seem to drain her o' no information, and I'm on the tanterhooks all the

time with the children mussin' over her silk
umbrell' and things.  Ha! ha! ye've found
a better mother than me, hain't ye, ye little
ongrate!" she said, good-naturedly, taking
back her unwilling infant.

As the dusk was growing, some one had
opened wide both doors; the wind swept
through, sweet and cool; children were
swinging across the aisle on suspended
shawl - straps; the conductor, making an
occasional entry, stepped obligingly over
both children and swings; seeing the place
beside Hebe empty, he sat down there.

The young carpenter was having another
serious conversation with his girl; he arose
and addressed something to the ears of the
passengers as he stepped down the aisle;
when he reached Margaret he paused in the
same grave manner—

"Will you join us in singing the 'Sweet
By-and-by'?"

Margaret's mouth twitched with the surprise of the invitation.

"I will do my best," she said.

The carpenter's girl started it, but Hebe

took it up and flooded the car with it; she
sang the first verse in a thrilling soprano;
she rendered the second in a showy alto;
she warbled the third in a melting tremulo,
" We shall meet on that beautiful shore."

The conductor, as temporary proprietor
of so much vocal pre-eminence, put his arm
engagingly along the back of Hebe's seat.

A man in sleek broadcloth, who had come
strolling from one of the first - class car-
riages, stood in the door and stared markedly at Hebe with insolent favor.

The conductor at length rose up reluc-
tantly and went about his duties.

The first-class man, after a brief absence,
returned and renewed his unembarrassed
gaze and waiting attitude at the door.
Hebe's head was thrown back; when would
the dove-like lids open again and conscious-
ly or unconsciously invite this unctuous new
admirer?

Margaret, impelled by a new, perhaps a
second-class, impulse of tenderness for what
did not concern her, walked leisurely and,
as it were, indifferently over to the girl.

"May I sit down here a moment?" she
said. "One gets so tired in the one place."

"Cert'nly," said Hebe, stiffly.

"That is my card," said Margaret, putting that choicely engraved and black-edged
memento in Hebe's hand. "Stuart. My
name was Stuart and I married a Stuart,
not a cousin either, not any relation—but it
was quite odd, was not it?" she went on,
with trained facility for making talk.

"I don't carry my name around except in
my head," said Hebe. "It's Milderd St.
Thomas. 'Duds Sen Tammy' they call me
over to Yarmouth."

"Do you live in Yarmouth? I am going
there."

"I work in the lobster factory—canning."
Mildred St. Thomas seemed to hope this
would prove shocking.

"We take the boat to-morrow?"

"Yes, and it's an awful cranky boat, too:
the wind's east, it's going to be rough."
Mildred spoke as though this at least should
settle her undesired acquaintance, and turned her head to the window.

"Am I incommoding you?" said Margaret, gently, after a little. "Would you rather have the seat for — other acquaintances?"

"I'm not pitch!" said Mildred St. Thomas, with a relieving flash of indignation. "If people come and stick to me, I can't help it; but I ain't a fool, and there's no pitch on me, either!"

Margaret sat very quiet, not even drawing away after this blow.

The first-class man in broadcloth had disappeared from view. The car was growing very dim, and there were yet no signs of lighting the lamps; mothers here and there were crooning their tired babies to sleep; and still the lady, silent and unoffended, sat close by the resentful member of the lobster factory.

"May I kiss you, dear?" she said, rising at last. "I am so lonely to-night—I can hardly keep from crying."

Mildred lifted a sudden wondering glance to the pale face and trembling lips above her. " *You* kiss *me!*" she laughed bit-

terly under her breath. Margaret stooped
down and kissed her, and the veil she wore
fell for an instant softly over the girl's
shoulder; then she went back to her place.

When the lamps were ablaze the traveller
in broadcloth came again and stood tentatively at the door, but Mildred's averted
face rested against the cushions, hopelessly
cold and unresponsive.

The matron disposed her sleeping children
wherever science, assisted by philanthropy,
could make room for them. One little fellow with home-knit woollen stockings, and
pink slippers from the shop, grew painfully
cramped and distressed in position as the
night wore on and his mother's unconscious
form became inattentive.

Margaret, sleepless, lifted him and laid him
easily in her own arms; one wild, strange
look he gave her, then instantly caught up
the thread of his broken slumbers with a
grateful sigh.

"Have you been holdin' that young one
all night, ma'am? God forgive me, I
couldn't no more help sleepin' than a cat

under a stove! God bless ye kindly, ma'am!
Do take my pocket-mirrer!"

It was thrice cracked. Margaret retained
it a moment, politely trying to find some
coherent plan of her features in it. Unsuccessful in this, she smoothed some strands of
hair as gravely as if the reflection had been
in any degree suggestive.

"Goin' on by boat?"

"Yes."

"Well, I ain't, thank the Lord! When
we get to Percy's Mount I'm home. Ye're
a proud-sized woman, but ye ain't over and
above robust lookin'. I invite ye kindly to
stop 'n' rest with me till Thursday's boat.
My man's dead, but I've always had a jant
o' meat in the house so far."

"No, thank you; I will go on."

"Anybody waitin' for ye?"

"No."

"Summerin'?"

"Summering and wintering, both," said
Margaret, with a catch in her throat the
other did not hear.

On the boat Margaret clung for life to

the cold wind of the deck; the craft pitched and rolled, and a dreadful premonition of illness was upon her. All had gone below save herself, braced amidships, and one other individual, leaning with plain disgust of life over the railing. In her sick despair she had not even noticed that it was the sleek first-class traveller of the train, now miserably collapsed, with his hat hanging at his side and his bald head revealed.

A steward ascended to sound the supper-gong in the ears of this feeble audience.

"Bring me a piece of salt codfish, un-cooked, and some pilot-bread," Margaret said to him, and a sick hallucination came to her that this repast, and this alone, could stay her woes.

But no sooner had she taken it in her hand than an uncontrollable desire came over her to throw it as far from her as possible into the sea. She knew that she could never reach the deck-railing, yet un-less that piece of fish were even in the depths of the sea she felt that she should die.

She had been called a straight and strong thrower, for a woman, but illness had already seized her; the codfish glanced forth, wavering, thwarted too by a gust of wind, and hit her suffering solitary companion on the back of his bald head!

Margaret leaned, clinging faintly with her slender straining muscles to a deck-chair in front of her; she half expected that evil missile to be hurled back at her, but was indifferent, and only remembered, for her own unprovoked attack, that all crimes are forgiven to the dying.

"You're so cold! — you ought to· come down" — it was Mildred's voice — "come down to your state-room!"

"I haven't any state-room; besides, if I leave the air I shall die!"

"I'll fix you all right—you sha'n't be sick any more. Let me help you. Come!"

Half carried by those strong young arms, Margaret found herself down the stairs in the lighted cabin, and flat on her back amid soothing pillows and blankets. Gentle hands relieved her of her bonnet and smoothed the hair from her aching temples, and she knew no more till morning.

"Say, we've struck Yarmouth; let's get off and beat the town for a lookin'-glass!"

"Oh, how good you have been to me!" cried Margaret, springing up, yet with something so blank and hopeless in her face.

Mildred drew nearer, hesitating, a strange softness in her voice: "Perhaps you're a stranger? Perhaps—you want a cheap place to live? Maybe—perhaps—you want something to do?"

Margaret's great eyes answered her.

"I'm a settled 'resident.'" The girl laughed. "I'll fix you all right. It's poor and cheap —the place I mean—but there ain't a shady thing in it nor by it; and—I'll find you something fit to do. I'm not working to-day—come! I feel like crusadin' 'round on just this shape of a racket." She gathered up Margaret's traps, laughing. "Look!" said she, merrily, as if to stave off the tears of gratitude in the other's eyes; "do you see that landor and coachman, and him gettin' in? That's the richest man in Yarmouth—that's the big Judson Sprague."

Margaret saw the wily flirt of the train, the miserable sufferer of the deck.

"He don't know me, but I know who he is," continued Mildred. "Oh, ain't he giddy, though, when he gets away from home!"

"I excelled him in sprightliness," said Margaret. "I hit him—on the head—with a good half pound of ossified codfish. The wind blew so—I was so ill—"

Mildred leaned her hands on her hips and laughed till she was weak. "Say, your 'reserved seat' 's all right, if you never do another good thing! Say, he's an old widower—you needn't 'a' been afraid I'd flirted with him. High-toned folks like you he's all right to, but poor girls like me are dirt under his feet; a try-to-kiss and a kick, that's his style with such as me, and your sort don't usually mind such as us bein' insulted. It's expected. But he's got a boy that ain't like him!" Mildred blushed frankly. "Jeff Sprague. I know him to speak to. Come on, now—we're goin' to fix you cosey."

## CHAPTER II

"Mrs. Margaret Stuart—Mrs. O'Ragan Stuart."

"Stuart, is it? Thank God, thin, we've the one name! and so I thought by the looks o' ye, darlin'. 'Tis a race ye can tell ony-wheres, begorry! Look forninst me wall!"

Margaret did so, and saw an engraving of the Scottish queen in her youth.

Mrs. O'Ragan, with the sleeves rolled up from her powerful arms and a large rope knotted aggressively about her waist, herself stood gazing in rapture.

"Will," said she, turning to Margaret, "would yez know us for the one family?"

"The resemblance is—something wonderful."

"Will, thin! blisséd saint that she was, that Quane Elizabeth put to the stroke! And what happened hersilf for doin' the same, but didn't she combusticate in her dith, so niver a flitherin of her could be found between the two says? Plontogonet, go and fitch the clar't dimmyjon. Fool wid the cork, and I'll fool wid yez!

"'Pleg' he's called for short," she added, gravely; "and more Pleg he is for short than long for Plontogonet.

"Take a sip, darlin'," said Mrs. O'Ragan, pouring a little into a glass. "'Tis the same I took bit by bit to Winny Hinchy beyant the yard, and 'twas the last sip she took jist afore she died, yisterday. Will yez wake wid us the night?"

"I've been waking for two nights," said Margaret, with unimpeachable solemnity, tasting the wine, however, under the compulsion of an inherited courtesy that could march to the death.

"Dear, thin, niver mind. We can't all be the one thing, and there's many a Bamboo that I love as will as I do me own." For it soon developed to Margaret's increasing intelligence that Mrs. O'Ragan had a convenient habit of calling every one who was not both Celtic in race and Roman Catholic in ritual a "Bamboo"—not with religious reprobation, but merely as relying on the term to convey a general sense of something foreign. Whether connected in her mind with Bombay or not was never definitely known.

"Thank you. May I go up to my rooms now?"

"Pleg, show the lady. They're airy, ma'am, on the side to the bluffs. Miss Duds Sen Tammy said you was one o' this kind must be always sippin' a bit o' frish air. Don't be wishful, ma'am, dear. The blisséd Mother o' God is wid us here and yon and iverywhere. Pleg!"

Plantagenet preceded Margaret up the stairs, indicated her apartments by turning and giving the door a stout kick with his bare foot, and rushed from her presence.

Margaret picked up the key, rattled to the floor by this procedure, and went in.

"The blessed Mother of God is with us here and yon and everywhere." The words came to her as she looked out on the bay with its green islands.

Within was a tiny kitchen, white in the sunlight, and adjoining a bedroom, bare as to wall and floor, the latter throwing up fretful splinters in retaliation for a recent scrubbing.

There stood her trunks, remnants of the labels of extensive foreign travel still adhering to them. Margaret bit her lip with an odd smile; the smile deepened to half-hysterical, solitary laughter at the incongruous quality of the contents, whose quiet, costly elegance lay revealed amid her surroundings. Replacing all save a few of the plainest, and one summer gown of purest white, daintily and choicely lace-trimmed, which she laid on top as if for a purpose, she closed the lid and answered a knock at the door.

" 'Tis dressed wid an onion it is, ma'am," cried Mrs. O'Ragan, delightedly holding out a piece of brown meat on a plate, "and knowin' yez haven't yet had time to be layin' in yer bits o' pervisions."

" You are too kind!" That the meat was clothed—even swathed—in onion was evident to more than one sense. Finding an

erratic knife and fork among her kitchen
furniture, Margaret proceeded to investi-
gate. Faint with hunger, she found the result strangely agreeable, and thus employed
was startled by another knock at the door.

"Call me always Agnaiz!" exclaimed
a wholesome, affectionate voice. Margaret
went into the bedroom to bring her other
chair—she had one for each room.

Agnes appeared not to notice that she
had been absent for that purpose, or that
there were other than twenty chairs in the
room.

"I have five childs," she said, seating herself, "and one husban'."

Margaret smiled back into the comely
foreign face.

"I live also here. I wailcome you! We
are Bamboos togezzer!" she added, laughing
with the most musical good-fellowship.

Her cotton dress was soiled and her hands
labor-worn, but she seemed a most serene
lady.

"My husban' is Irishmans. Well, he *iss*
so good. Wait till I tell you. 'Agnaiz,' he

says to me, 'everyt'ing ever you weesh I
give it you, and all the time you leef wid
me I never seen you cry—now you cry because I been drinkin' some liquors. Go put
on your t'ings and come 'long wid me.' So
we went, and he sign de pladge! Now,
dare!"

"That is splendid!"

"Yas, is it not? I love mans."

This was a little startling.

"Young mans!"

Margaret looked up and met a pair of
pure dark eyes gazing seriously at her from
Agnes's face.

"One has also here a room. He was var'
ill. I save him from dine. I love him as
my own childs—but he is Jew!"

Agnes lifted her eloquent eyes and crossed
herself, sorrowfully.

"Now I love you, too," she added.

"And I am neither Jew nor Catholic,"
said Margaret, smiling.

"I care not. Somet'ing to my heart says
I shall meet you and Isaak in dose better
worl's. Have you a nutmaig, Miz' Stuart?"

Now, strangely, Margaret had seen this
very article, overlooked by a former tenant,
in a corner of the kitchen shelf, and she
brought it. Agnes blushed her most gracious thanks, and rising soon thereafter, unfolded from a damask napkin a loaf of cake,
than which Margaret had never seen anything more alluringly toothsome in appearance.

"Dis mornin'," said Agnes, inconsequent-
ly, laying the loaf in its white napkin on the
table, "I mek' a cake. You are yet so busy,
I baig you to accep' my poor meeserable
loaf of cake."

"I do not know how to thank you!"

"Come to see me. I shall mek' you always 'appy; so shall my husban' and childs.
Isaak—that is Jew young mans—shall come
in an' play you 'armony, and I shall sing
you."

She went out. "She saw the nutmeg and
asked for it," thought Margaret, "so that
she could more easily give me the cake. I
have stumbled on a queer community,"
she continued, musing; "they seem to have

a mania for giving! I must return these favors. But I have heard that 'tenement' people are always borrowing of and lending to one another, and *that* is demoralizing," she concluded, shivering a little righteously under the spell of superior traditions. "I shall treat them well — I cannot, of course, really associate with them—but I shall neither lend nor borrow."

Seldom had a good resolution earlier opportunity for enforcement.

A third rap at the door, and a tall, thin woman, with a great fund of humor in her eye, and a very small Derby hat capping jauntily a person otherwise unrecovered from the dishabille of the kitchen, made her appearance.

"I'm Mrs. Shaughnessy," she said, with much hope.

"My name is Stuart," replied Margaret, rather coldly.

"Yes, Mrs. O'Ragan was jist tellin' me ye were her own cousin belike."

Margaret blushed violently, but did not speak.

"Ye're lookin' very fine, ma'am. If ever there's onything I can do for ye, jist come to the landin' an' pound wid yer petaty-masher. I'm on the upper floor correspondin'. Could ye, Mrs. Stuart, ma'am, be loanin' me a half-dizzen petatys till mornin'?"

"I am very sorry," said Margaret (who was very glad), "but I have not yet purchased any potatoes." This last clause being the pellucid truth.

"What! not a petaty? God help ye, ma'am," cried Mrs. Shaughnessy, fervently; "that sha'n't long be said o' ye!" And she shot away.

"I will go out and get some things," said Margaret to herself, testily, locking the door, "as soon as I can take my bath and change my dress."

These things she accomplished with the elaborate leisure of super-refined habit. "My soiled clothing!" she said, with a new thought, eying it in dismay. "Of course I shall have to get a tub and do them myself;" and she folded them away, not without a smack of conscious savor in the originality of this enterprise.

With gentle leisure, too, she adjusted her bonnet, hesitated gracefully, as usual, which wrap to put on, and was sailing out—a disproportionate figure—through her wee kitchen, when there came another rap—a courteously firm one.

"I am very anxious about you," said a slight young man, the sorrows of Israel in his dark eyes, and bowing as he handed Margaret an irreproachable card. "I am a friend of Mrs. Agnes Sullivan."

"Will you come in?" said Margaret, with small animation, and leaving the door to the dingy hall wide open.

"I will detain you but a moment; you are going out." He accepted one of the chairs. Margaret, sitting in the other, her choice black draperies sweeping the bare little floor, blushed with annoyance.

But no sense of these things affected the earnest and grave consciousness of Isaac Gilchrist; his prophetic eyes took in no puny detail.

"I simply wish to say," he went on, "that
you must remember always that you have
friends—dear and loving friends—of whom
I am one. You must not let yourself be
afraid. Remember, always, there is one in
this house who thinks of you."

He rose to go. "I thank you," said Margaret, biting her lip, nor wholly able to con-
ceal the irreverent amaze in her eyes. This
expression widened to frank and mirthful
scepticism as she closed the door after her
guest.

"He *is* the 'Wandering Jew'—at last!"
with a gleam of her beautiful white teeth
that there was no one near to appreciate;
"his face is about thirty, his eyes—witnessed
the erection of the pyramids! 'A dear and
loving friend! thinking always of one!' and
with no more capacity for coquetry than the
stone tablets of the law! Well, as Mrs.
O'Ragan's 'own cousin,' I must be going
out for me petatys."

Margaret stepped charily down the stairs
and out. Hesitating a moment whether to
follow the attractive path along the bluffs,

or to go immediately to the town, she saw a much-encumbered figure toiling up the street.

With a glad leap in her heart she went to meet Mildred St. Thomas.

"I'm used to these things. I c'n make better bargains 'n you," said the handsome girl, beaming erect amid her numerous parcels. "The coals are coming right along."

"Oh, how lovely of you! Coals—to be sure! I never thought."

So the two went up to the little kitchen, and putting the small receipted bills together made up the sum with brows indicating intense application, and Margaret gratefully reimbursed her friend.

"Now stay to tea with me; stay!" she said, bustling about housewifely.

"I guess I will, for your sake, if you're going to cook the meat that way," said Mildred. "Mrs. Cap'n"—she burst out laughing.

"What?"

"Mrs. Cap'n Herkimer's coming up to see you to-morrow morning. She"— Mildred choked somewhat again—"w-wants you to help her."

"Why are you laughing so? Housework?"

"N-no.  It's b-brain-work."

"Well, perhaps I am not so deficient as you think," said Margaret, with slight asperity, putting an iron kettle in her dish-pan and proceeding to wash the soot off the bottom.

"People don't do that.  They don't wash the bottoms of kettles like that."

"They must be very indecent then," said Margaret, with a fine virtue that nevertheless was already beginning to merge into despair.

"See here! you've got in a rocky place. You'll never see a rockier," said Mildred, gently usurping the stand at the sink.

Margaret, with red cheeks, spent some ten minutes in restoring her arms and hands to their original complexion.

"What made you laugh so in speaking of Mrs. Captain Herkimer?"

"Oh, n-nothing.  I went to see her—she'll be up to-morrow."

"Is she a fool that wishes another fool for company?" said Margaret, discovering another streak of soot on her fair wrist.

Mildred simply gave her a jovial, rather reproachful, glance out of her bright brown eyes.

"Come and sit with me just for a little, dear — I'm so lonely. We will put some coals on the grate in my bedroom."

Mildred watched the older woman's tranquil position, the graceful ease of her quiet hands, the sweep of her soft dress on the splintered floor, and half idolized her, and, half, her heart broke over her.

Mildred's own hands, used to "job-work" at the canning factory, clasped her knee restlessly.

"Tell me some more about those places where you have been, some time," she said, earnestly, when she rose to go; for Margaret's conversation, though only of the past, had been made vivid with interest for the girl, and Mildred St. Thomas had asked no questions.

"Wait a moment!" said Margaret, lightly,

going to the trunk where she had laid the white dress and lifting the lid. "I want you to take this—you would look so sweet in it of a summer day; not"— she said, glancing at the girl's face—"to pay you for being so kind to me—I could never do that —but because *I* wish you to have it."

"I can't take that!" said Mildred, looking down with burning eyes and cheeks where the exquisite, spotless thing lay unfolded. "I love it! I love those kind of things— but they ain't my sort! I can't take that!"

Margaret, who was used to having her own way, simply laid her head down on the trunk and put her hands to her face without a word.

"I'll take it," said Mildred, under this aspect of the affair. "Perhaps some time I'll be fit to—perhaps some time I can wear it."

"Why of course you will wear it," said Margaret, now brightly, wrapping up the gown.

The girl's face was pale; the lids had their dovelike droop, white and still. "Perhaps, some time."

Margaret kissed her, and she went out with her parcel.

At the third turn down the lighted street, Jeff Sprague showed his homely, beaming face. "Why, you're late to-night, Duds! Let me carry your parcel."

"You can't touch it!"

Jeff tried to find a securer resting-place for a small polo-cap on his particularly big head of coarse brown hair.

"Well, never mind. Some time you won't need to go about picking up old clothes," he said, with lurking tenderness in the jest.

"The old clothes where I got this — I'd wear her *rags*, I'd wear her cast-off shoes, sooner than I'll go with you any more, Jeff Sprague!"

"Why, Duds! Why, Mildred!"

"You're engaged to Nell Herkimer, and her folks don't know that you ever spoke a word to me. They was good to me when I went to get work for Mrs. Stuart — Nellie and all. I ain't on the square with 'em, and I don't like it!"

Jeff put his hands in his pockets and stood

with legs firmly planted, as if he were compelling the deck in a choppy sea. "I'll go and
tell Nellie to-night that I made a mistake—
that I ain't fit to make her happy. I'll go
to-night and tell my father that I'm going
to marry Mildred St. Thomas — a girl he
doesn't know, but whom, all the same, I'm
*going* to marry, and by to-morrow you shall
know that I have done both."

"Well—go then!"

Jeff's face lighted unreservedly. He started off.

"Jeff! Come back, Jeff! I'm not ready
yet, Jeff. I — I was just trying to see if
you are honest instead of a flirt like your
father. Your father tried to flirt with me
on the train, Jeff."

"I can't blame him; but the old boy's too
snobbish to marry a shop-girl, my darling—
all the better luck! I wouldn't have you
for a 'mamma'—neither for a mamma nor a
sister."

Mildred laughed, but with an absorbing
triumph in her eyes.

"I knew you were honest, Jeff—I knew.

But Nellie — she thinks you are honest, too."

"I am! I haven't kissed her once since I got acquainted with you. She thinks it's only 'backsliding.' I've told you times enough how her folks and my father hatched up that match, and she got me into a meeting—and cried. And—I was younger then. It was before you came." Jeff set his teeth, then sighed drearily. "But we'll work out of it all right, my girl. It's all bound to clear!"

"And she loves you?"

"How can she?" Evidently Jeff was incredulous that more than one girl could love him, if so much. Standing about the height of Mildred herself, his broad form was roughly muscular, his irregularly featured face looked almost grotesque in contrast with hers.

"But she might like ugly things, the same as me," said Mildred, pushing back one of the stiff locks under his cap, quite in the way of natural possession, a look in her face that struck Jeff as something to be holily regarded.

"But I believe in beauty in the family," he said, " and I'm going to have it !"

Mildred laughed condescendingly, as she would with an awkward child.

" Well, I can't have you walking with me any farther.   Good-night, Jeff !"

"It's a rocky world and a blind road, I must say," said the poor girl in her own room, spreading out Margaret's entrancing gift again to view.  She bent over it, touched the soft lace, and inhaled the dainty perfume still clinging to it, before putting it sacredly away.

"But Jeff—why, I *love* poor Jeff!  He's just my own boy like, Jeff is, and I'm all alone !"

" Well, it's rocky !"  Mildred's mattress was not calculated to soften her aspersions on life.

She had not knelt beside her bed, for that was not her habit, but after lying a long time with wide-open eyes, she put up her hands and forced the lids down, smarting :

" O God ! help me some time to be fit to wear the dress."

## CHAPTER III

"I HEAR you have a personage in these tenements," said Mrs. Captain Herkimer, severe in rustling silk.

"And pray what am I meself, ma'am?" inquired Mrs. O'Ragan.

"You used to do washing for me very well — very well, Bridget; but if you have by chance a refined person in reduced circumstances come to lodge here, I should advise you to take away that old broom that I've seen ricketin' up against the side o' the house since time was."

"Thank ye for yer complimint, ma'am, and the broom 'll stand there jist the same. There's nothing in an innercent old broom, swept clane wid mony a storm and wid a white rag flyin' to it for dark nights, to disagree wid yer meddlin', thavin' old Board o' Hilth, ma'am."

"Of course she's a Protestant, Bridget?"

"Why of course, thin? Yez have the social tact on ye, begorry, to come and insult me on me own door-stip!"

"Well, well, step aside, I'm coming in, Bridget." Mrs. Herkimer held up her dress, Bridget tightened the cable about her waist.

"I know you don't have unwholesome dirt, but you always have so many rags and tags lying about, Bridget. If you spent the time picking up that you spend going to that foolish 'mass,' raking and scraping all you can get together to get somebody's soul out o' purgatory—"

"Miz' Herkimaire!" cried an excited voice down the stairway, "on your *dine bed*, your sins look to you big as dis house!"

"Good-morning, Agnes," said Mrs. Herkimer, pleasantly.

"Once," continued Agnes, "I went, discusted, to your meeting. I hear get up a convert, an old lady. 'I smokes, I chews,' she says. 'Boo hoo!—for me pray'—while de boys do wads of paper at her t'row. I seen it!"

"It is Mrs. Herkimer!" gasped Margaret
to herself, hearing these turmoils. "Where
shall I place her in these bare rooms?" Not
shame, but the inherited sense of luxury,
made her stand suddenly aghast like one
uncovered.

But now a fresh commotion on all sides
arose, a noise and tumult that drowned the
renewed altercation of the captain's lady
and Mrs. O'Ragan, and into Margaret's bedroom came pouring the choicest furniture of
the tenements:

Mrs. Shaughnessy's two upholstered crim-
son plush chairs—"Oh, do, ma'am, jist while
ye be havin' yer call! Sure, our Blisséd
Saviour tells us to lind."

Agnes Sullivan's pretty rugs on the floor—
"It is our 'abit. Our Fader in heaven says
we shall always borrow one anodder."

A blue-silk counterpane from somewhere
else, pillow-covers standing out with starched
ruffles a quarter of a yard wide, glory, color
everywhere, and Margaret alone again, trying to bite back the tears. "And I would
not have loaned even a potato — on princi-

ple! Perhaps among the poor, it *is*—it *is* sometimes advisable!"

"Bridget," said Mrs. Herkimer's voice, on the third stair, "here's a button off of one of your boys' trousers. A button saved is a button earned, Bridget."

"Thank ye!" replied Mrs. O'Ragan, sarcastically. "Are ye sure it ain't the 'Christian Indivor' badge dropped off yerself, ma'am?"

"Pshaw! Bridget. You need a skewer to get the dirt out of these little corners here."

"Kape the button and welcome!" cried Mrs. O'Ragan, wrathfully; "it'll do well to dhrop for the support o' yer own church nixt Sunday, where, begorry, they pass around a smeltin'-net for a conthribution-box!"

The rustling silk entered Margaret's apartment.

"Well, you look quite comfortable here, Mrs. Stuart."

There were tears still in Margaret's eyes and red in her cheeks; she was not very comfortable, but she welcomed the captain's lady graciously.

"Mildurd St. Thomas (Mildurd's a girl that's sewed for me sometimes when she was off work at the cannin' factory) tells me you're a personage that wants something to do."

"Yes, I'll be glad of anything to do."

Now Margaret could no more help her voice being sweet and—lazy, than she could help the air of self-possession enveloping her.

"I see," said Mrs. Herkimer, contemplating her through her glasses—"I see." For a long time she saw, while Margaret gazed politely and composedly at the grate. "I know crosses myself. When captain and I was voyagin', I met with wreck once. We don't cruise now. We're very comfortable. Captain was on the seas at a time when sailin'-vessels made money. Yes, I suppose there ain't but one bigger house in Yarmouth, and that's Judson Sprague's.

"Ain't it hard, after all I've been through, that there ain't a soul to sympathize and feel with me?—nobody to set down and pet me a little? Dr. Saxe said the other day, 'Why,

Mrs. Herkimer, what you need's a little pettin',' he says."

The large and kindly eyes of the captain's lady were raised in mournful questioning to Margaret.

" Yes," said Margaret, vaguely.

" I feel if I could have some refined and interestin' person around a good part o' the time for company, it would do me more good than all the medicines. What's your opinion of prices ?"

" Oh," said Margaret, blushing warmly, "I should think it would hardly be worth anything !"

" *I* should consider it of some importance if I could be consoled and sympathized with a little. Still, I should want you to have dinner and supper with us, and as I require no manual labors of you—not even sewin'— nor constant attentions I should not desire, but only just to have ye around, so I could get at ye when I want ye. What do you say to seven cents an hour—fifty-six cents a day ?"

" I consider it extremely generous."

"I should wish you to stay stormy nights—
I'm always particularly lonely then, thinkin'
o' the sea—or on any particular occasions."

"I would stay."

"And now, can you begin to-day, Mrs.
Stuart—put on your things and drive me
home? Eulalie's fastened down in the street.
Captain drove me, but he has business to
stay in town, and he said you, being a young
woman, could probably steer me home."

"Certainly, I can drive." But Margaret
did not yet know The Meanest Horse that
Ever Lived. Eulalie, rough, lean of neck
and corpulent of stomach, stood in the shafts
of a smart phaeton, half of an evil eye cocked
over her blinder discriminatingly at Margaret
as she came down the path. Margaret, with
some experience and an instinctive appreciation of horse-flesh, regarded that eye and
form and sighed.

"She is well tied," she said, tentatively,
fingering a labyrinth of ropes.

"Yes," said Mrs. Herkimer, climbing into
the vehicle. "Captain turned her round and
headed her for home, and she *needs* tyin'

under them circumstances. When you get
to the last knot, you want to make quick
step to the carriage, or she'll go off and leave
ye."

Margaret sprang the last knot warily, and
rushed, only to go down the street, poised
like an acrobat, on the carriage step. Panting, she gained her seat, and Mrs. Herkimer
handed her the lines.

"*Now* you want to *saw* on her," said the
captain's lady, with dignified admonition,
for Eulalie, under these auspices, had gained
a rattling rate of speed. Margaret sawed
energetically, and, with a flirt of her tail
that said, "I'll have you later on," Eulalie
subsided into a fickle trot, and a little later
into an indomitable walk.

"She'll start up fast enough when she sees
the watering-trough in the square," said Mrs.
Herkimer; and indeed at the first glimpse
of that prospective basin, the unlovely beast's
every fibre became imbued with a stony im-
petus of self-will. Leaning far forward, and
wrenching the bit from side to side of the
creature's sin - hardened mouth, Margaret

brought up at the tub with a mere side clearing of one shaft, and Eulalie bent her head to drink. Margaret's silent prayer was that she would there drink until she died. This, though swelling visibly with watery greed, Eulalie refused to do.

"You done very well," said Mrs. Herkimer. "She's broke three shafts on captain."

Margaret's eyes were big and her face white. "What will she do next?" she inquired with exceeding calm, straightening her gloves.

"You don't need no particular directions now till you get to the home turn; only saw her down when she gets to goin' too fast."

Thus with alternate snail-pace and frenzy they came to a hill. Eulalie stopped, turned her head around, and regarded them with decision. "We've got to walk up," sighed Mrs. Herkimer, descending. "Sometimes she'll claw right up it."

"She'll claw right up it with *me* to-day!" said Margaret, taking out the whip, a mad joy in her eyes.

"Well, now, dear Mrs. Stuart, I'd just as

soon she wouldn't spoil my carriage. Captain's tried it. She only just stands and kicks."

"Very well," said Margaret, alighting, and taking Eulalie by the bit. Eulalie snapped at her. Margaret lifted her gloved hand and gave her a ringing slap across the snout, after which mutual expressions of regard they toiled up the hill together.

"Do you like her?" said Margaret, after desperately staying the brute for Mrs. Herkimer's reseating, and taking another acrobatic race on the carriage stirrup.

"Oh yes; I think a horse is safer that you're on the lookout for; then you ain't ever taken off your guard. You'll like her when you get to know her. There's nothin' like knowing a horse. You want to be careful, takin' the turn to the driveway; she's apt to *slew* there."

If slewing consisted in rounding the curve on the two right wheels of the vehicle while the other two whizzed spherically in air, Eulalie certainly accomplished that object in spite of Margaret's exertions. At the door she stopped with a suddenness that considerably assisted Mrs. Herkimer in her descent, and Margaret stepped down breathless.

"I think," said she, in that fine, languid voice of hers, and leaning up against the first convenient object—"I think, Mrs. Herkimer, I've earned—earned my first seven cents!" The voice broke in merriment.

Mrs. Herkimer glanced up, at first wonderingly, then slowly dropped her parcels and laughed till the tears rolled down her cheeks.

"Helen," said she to a grave beauty who appeared in the doorway, "this is Mrs. Stuart. I don't know when I've been chirked up so!"

Helen gave Margaret's hand a shy but homely clasp.

"Now follow me, Mrs. Stuart." Through velvet drawing-rooms Margaret followed the majestic tread of the captain's lady, and up a wide staircase. "There is your room, to wash your hands or arrange your hair, or when you stay overnight."

It was a very handsome room, but the imp that sometimes took possession of Margaret's eyes shone broad in them still, and meeting them Mrs. Herkimer yielded again to the subtle instinct of laughter.

"Really, something's chirked me up amazin'! Wander around till dinner-time where ye like, Mrs. Stuart: get acquainted with the premises. That," she added, in her former sombre tone, " was my only child—my daughter Helen."

" I thought her charming," said Margaret, now quite earnestly.

" She's a good girl. She's engaged to marry Jeffrey Sprague."

" Yes, I've heard the name."

"She's melancholic. It's in the family. I had a brother drowned himself. He left me thirty thousand dollars. You'll see the well when you go out."

Mrs. Herkimer's eyes were pitiful. Margaret looked a sympathy she could not speak.

" I hope Jeffrey 'll pet her. Captain's a good man, but he don't understand how much folks need pettin' sometimes."

Margaret wandered about the grounds, but she had a secret sense that Mrs. Herkimer was watching from a window to see if she noticed the well; so she went and leaned pensively on the curb.

In the same fashion, at the dinner-table, as the captain's lady lifted her glass, Margaret looked and saw her tearful eyes fixed appealingly upon her.

"How long since you lost your brother?" she inquired, in tender tones.

"Three years—but of course this always reminds me—"

"Nonsense!" interposed Captain Herkimer. "I never think on't! He wa'n't in there but three hours, and we had it all pumped out. Where 'd yer get this meat?"

"I got it at the most expensive place in town, Captain Herkimer."

"Ye might just as well 'a' gone where 'twas cheap," said the captain, sawing, even as one was required to saw upon the bit of the malignant Eulalie.

Mrs. Herkimer glanced knowingly at Mar-

4

garet, as much as to say, "Is it not as I told
you?"

There was an air of gloom over the table,
to which Helen, the daughter, seemed naturally to assent, but the captain chafed.

"Eat the greens, then," said Mrs. Herkimer, solemnly; "they're better food for ye,
now that your workin'-days are over."

"By God!" said the captain, still sawing,
"bring home such a piece o' meat as this,
and then say my workin'-days are over!" and
he laughed in defiance of the whole board.

"Mrs. Stuart," said the captain's lady, referring her directly to another guest at the
table, a chance visitor—"Mrs. Cap'n Roberts
is sitting in the very chair that her husband
set in last time he was to this house before
he died o' heart disease. She was sitting
in it in the west parlor before dinner, and
I had it brought out for her. She comes
sometimes to set in it."

"Captain Roberts was a good man," said
Captain Herkimer, with cheerful sincerity.
"He wouldn't have joined in with any such
dumbed nonsense."

"Captain Herkimer, are you a Methodist?"

"I am."

"Oh, I was under the impression that maybe you was a free-thinker!"

"So I be. Have some blueberry sauce, Tilly," said he, winking engagingly at Mrs. Roberts's little girl.

"I'm sick of blueberry sauce," replied the little girl, despondently; "we have it all the time to home."

Meanwhile Mrs. Roberts had been holding her handkerchief to her eyes. Mrs. Herkimer now looked desperately at Margaret, as one who was even under stipend to console.

"It is very sad," said the latter, tasting the actual bitterness of a small daisy that had mingled with her greens—"it is very sad," she went on, biting her sweet lips, "to lose any one so dear in so sudden—"

"Say, Nell," said the captain to his wife, triumphantly dancing a trio of burdocks on the blade of his knife, "do you think that colored lady you've got in the kitchen understands sortin' greens?"

"She belongs to the same church you and
I do, Captain Herkimer."

"Why, Nell! Why, what the devil," said
the Captain reasonably and argumentative-
ly—"what difference does it make what
church she belongs to, her sortin' greens?"

"I have said what I have said."

"I know ye have, and I wish to thunder
there was more sense to it. What ye go'n'
to have for dessert?"

"Our dessert to-day you'll soon see. What
our final dessert is to be—" Mrs. Herkimer
paused with excess of meaning. "Life is
short," she at length concluded.

"Wall, I'm glad there's *somethin'* short,"
said Captain Herkimer, without a sigh, "for
I'm darned sure this gingerbread ain't!"

In the awful silence that followed, some
thing occurred—*the sad little girl giggled.*

The captain's face broke into approving
smiles. "That's right, Tilly! You and I
ain't got hypochondry, have we? Come,
ladies," said he, straightening his fine figure,
after having made, in spite of these unflat-
tering digressions, a very wholesome and

satisfactory meal, "the tide serves.  Put on
your things, and come down for a sail."

IIelen's dark eyes lifted for the first time
with a gleam of joy.

"Presently, captain," said Mrs. Herkimer,
gravely concealing her own elation.  "We'll
go up to the cupola first and get weighed
and take the view."

"Gad! do ye weigh yer company *afore*
dinner, too?" chuckled the captain.  But Mrs.
Herkimer proceeded to lead to the execution
of these rites with unaffected solemnity.

CHAPTER IV

"THROUGH all my trials and sufferin's,"
said Mrs. Herkimer, with significant reproach in the direction of the captain, "I've
never been petted before; but Mrs. Stuart
understands me."

"*She* pet ye!" said the captain. "She's all
o' thirty years younger 'n you be!"

"*Sympathy* is somethin' that, if it ain't
given to you by nature, you may be as gray
as a snow-storm" (now the captain's curly
head was gray) "and still you won't have
it."

A particularly handsome old dog rose up
at the doorway and prepared to follow them.

"No, Stack, you can't go!" said Mrs. Herkimer, with a firmness not calculated to be
gainsaid. "You'll be jumping out o' the
boat into the water, and then coming back
and shakin' it all over us."

Stack looked at her with his sublime brown eyes, too noble for resentment, too sad and loving for reproach, and lay down again.

But, lo! as they took the path around the corner of the lawn, there, with genial welcome, and nothing sneakish in his expression, stood Stack waiting.

"Captain Herkimer, make that dog go home!"

"Go home, Stack!"

Stack turned his huge frame with unoffended dignity and trotted back.

They went along the road and turned into the lane, and there, on the other side of the bars, his face of solemn, loving congratulation turned full towards them, again stood Stack, waiting.

"Captain Herkimer, can you be obeyed by your own dog?"

"Stack! Go home!" thundered the captain.

Again Stack gravely turned and disappeared.

The big boat was anchored at some little

distance in the bay; the dory for passage
to it waited on the beach, and when they
reached this latter and looked out, there, up-
right beside the main-mast, gazing fondly
and expectantly towards them, sat Stack.

"He's swum out to her?" said the captain,
delightedly.

"You'd ought to had a large family to
bring up," said his lady, with serene sarcasm; "it's a pity to have such trainin' gifts
as yours wasted!"

But it was perfectly evident that the ti-
rade about Stack had been a mere formality, and that both these partners in life's
joys were equally satisfied with his adventure.

"Ye're pretty hefty women. I'll paddle
ye over one to time," said the captain. "She's
a little dory, and she leaks. Set square amidships, Nell."

"If I'd sailed to the world's end with ye
a few more times than what I have, Captain
Herkimer, perhaps I'd need instructions how
to set in a dory."

The captain sculled, and the majestic form

of Mrs. Herkimer was soon descried sitting beside Stack.

"Now, Mrs. Stuart," said the captain, lifting the dory at one end and letting out a cataract of water on the beach, "set just where Mrs. Herkimer did, and do jest as I tell ye, and don't worry. I shall get ye over afore she fills."

Calmly taking her life in her hand, as it seemed to her, at seven cents an hour, Margaret stepped in. The race was exciting, and the result appeared doubtful. She wrapped her skirts about her and put her feet on the box in front of her, as she had seen Mrs. Herkimer do, while the green surges of the sea lapped ever higher against the sides of the dory.

The captain, with his back towards her, stood erect, wielding one oar, and as he brought up alongside the boat, Margaret rose with the intention of getting aboard with as little delay as possible, but the dory gave an unexpected lurch; she caught wildly at the captain's coat-tails—

"What in hell ye doin'?" cried he, as they

were both precipitated to the bilgy floor of
the dory. "Never mind," he added, with
tender apology, on recovering himself, "the
salt water won't hurt ye. But ye came pretty near capsizin' us. Now wait, and do jest
as I say. I want ye always to wait my
word when ye're seafarin' with me."

"I will," said Margaret, climbing over into
the boat with the meek look of one who has
suffered watery eclipse.

But Mrs. Herkimer sat convulsed with silent laughter. As one who has sailed the
seas, and is conversant with all the devices
of that lore, Margaret's performance appealed
most keenly to her sense of the ludicrous.
She tried to stem her mirthful tears, but
could not.

"I seem very successful in chirking you
up," said Margaret, languidly and sweetly.
But Stack came over to the humiliated one,
his coat still dripping, and shook the salt
water over those portions of her garments
not yet submerged, and looked up at her
gravely, straightforwardly, so great a measure of valiant love in his human—truer than

human — eyes that Margaret instinctively reached out her hand and laid it on his head. He steadily composed himself beside her, and there remained.

When the "tacking" sail struck her hat off, Stack lifted it to her in his mouth with sublime expression, and its tooth-indented surface suffered nothing in her estimation thereby.

"How beautifully you steer!" she said to Helen.

"She minds the hellum as well as I do!" said Captain Herkimer.

"I love it!" said the girl in a low tone, with glowing eyes, to Margaret—"I love it so, I think sometimes I ought not to come, just to try myself."

"Nonsense, child! Isn't this wind strong enough to blow such misconceptions out of your head?"

"Why," said the girl, very sadly, after a pause, "aren't you a Christian?"

"Yes, surely," said Margaret, smiling.

"And don't you deny yourself things you love?"

"Nothing legitimate—that I can get."

Stack thumped his tail appreciatively on the floor. Mrs. Herkimer turned—"You've got a friend that 'll stand by you now," she said, indicating Stack.

"He doesn't laugh at me," said Margaret.

This opened afresh the fountains of Mrs. Herkimer's mirth. But Margaret had an unsought revenge when, later, as they two were wending their way homeward up the lane together, she climbed lightly over the fence, and was proceeding to put down the bars for the captain's lady.

"I prefer to climb it," said the latter, with solid dignity.

She was very stout, and reached the top rail laboriously. There the progress of her adventures became uncertain, and she sat, fearfully poised, a limb on either side.

"Let yourself down gently right into my arms," said Margaret, "I am strong."

"When I come, I mean to come altogether," replied Mrs. Herkimer. "No; I wish you, Mrs. Stuart, to climb up here and steady that other foot over; then I can descend."

Margaret did so, but as they both sat thus deliberating and wrestling on the fence, a victoria, drawn by two horses with gold-mounted harnesses, came richly tinkling down the lane.

"Let me assist you, ladies, I beg," said the unctuous voice of the elder Sprague.

Margaret, without assistance, was on *terra firma* in an instant. Mrs. Herkimer solemnly committed herself to the arms of the richest man in Yarmouth.

"I am passing your way, and I beg that you will do me the honor," said he, animatedly pointing the way to the carriage.

"I will walk with Stack, thank you," said Margaret.

"I wish you to accompany me," said Mrs. Herkimer, in a resonant whisper. "I have something to say, and I need you to support me through it."

Blushing madly—at seven cents an hour—Margaret followed Mrs. Herkimer into the carriage, where the latter sat as though it belonged to her.

"How old was your wife when she died,

Judson?" said she, gravely, without other
initiative.

"Ah—sixty; yes, sixty—a few months
over, Mrs. Herkimer."

"I was indisposed at the time, but I've
heard that ye had young men only—boys
atween eighteen and twenty—for pall-bear-
ers!"

"Ah—yes; a fancy. Just a fancy, Mrs.
Herkimer."

"*It's a fancy I don't approve of in ye.*"

This was the ordeal Mrs. Herkimer had
anticipated, and in which she had required
Margaret to sustain her.

The autocrat of Yarmouth colored, and
looked at the younger woman with humor-
ous, disagreeably insinuating, sweetness.

Margaret bit her lip with conflicting emo-
tions and looked away.

"Since you are staying at Yarmouth, Mrs.
Stuart," said the urbane gentleman, assisting
them to alight, "may I have the pleasure of
calling upon you?"

"I—I am working. I do not receive calls."

"Do not say so. Ah, too bad—too bad,

I assure you. Remember—ah—remember you made the 'first advances,'" he warned her, with a sort of caressing laughter.

"I beg your pardon for that—I was ill— I had no intention"—said Margaret, in a quicker tone than usual, remembering, indeed, painfully the fishy missile with which she had once assailed him.

"Ah, yes; but it struck—it struck home," he murmured, with his back well turned towards Mrs. Herkimer, and laying his plump hand on the region of his heart.

"I am very glad, at least, if I left a 'good impression,'" said Margaret, showing her white teeth a trifle maliciously; and she walked away, giving room to Mrs. Herkimer, who was uneasily waiting to convey some other admonition to her mature friend.

Margaret walked up the path. The Meanest Horse that Ever Lived, who was allowed free range of the premises, and of the universe, too, for that matter, stood directly athwart it. When Margaret, avoiding her heels, attempted a semicircular movement in front of her, she steadily moved forward, grazing with assumed innocence.

Margaret, who had wished to make a dignified retreat, now heard the flowery Sprague approaching. "Sho! sho!" he cried, waving his silk hat. Eulalie glanced at him, and with a loud squeal and a backward thrust of her heels, shot at a mad and wholly unnecessary gallop out of sight.

Margaret, with hot cheeks and bursting sensations, walked beyond the house, where Stack lay on the lawn in the sun. She sat down beside him, trembling with laughter. Stack did not laugh, but only looked a benign indulgence. She took a piece of pound-cake from her pocket, that Mrs. Herkimer had given her for her luncheon, and began to feed him. Stack was fond of pound-cake, and dainties were rare with him now; for, in view of his advanced years, the captain had brought home a new puppy to take his place when he should be gone.

Stack had accepted this fact, of his own volition, with a quietness and magnanimity exceeding much conduct that is called "Christian." Margaret had seen, when the plate of scraps was set outside the door for the two, how the great dog waited for the adolescent—about a tenth of his own size—to consume the choicest, and only when he turned away satiated made his own meal of the remains, with the lofty indifference of a sage.

"I am going to save you the nicest of everything I have, anywhere. I am going to get you some splendid pieces of meat," said Margaret, putting her arm around his shaggy neck.

" Oh, how sweet you are! But don't rob yourself," said the brown eyes in return.

"I love to sit here with you. I love to watch the sea—at just about this distance, Stack."

" Oh, but you need not fear; I could save you if you fell in. I've saved people before —I could do it again. I'm that breed."

" Yes, I believe you would." She gently twisted some of his hair into fantastic shapes, but Stack looked sublime under all circumstances.

5

When she went towards the house she was surprised at the excessive kindness in the captain's face. "I shall never have another dog like him, Mrs. Stuart," said he, in a genuinely tremulous voice; "but I had to get the puppy, ye see. Stack's old, and when—"

"Oh, hush!" said Margaret. "Don't say it before *him!*"

Mrs. Herkimer, too, in reckoning up her day's wage, beamed upon her like a mother.

"But I haven't really earned it," said Margaret. "I'm sure I sat with Stack, just loafing, a whole hour in the sun."

"I shouldn't want ye if ye didn't set with Stack," said Mrs. Herkimer, solemnly; "he's our friend." Then, as a last evidence of her chirking up for the day, her lip began to quiver. "Did Judson Sprague propose to ye?"

"Not definitely; he only intimated that his heart was open for attack."

"I really don't think he's nothing worse than an old fool."

"That is hopeful."

"Jeff's sensible and plain—like his mother."

"I should think it likely, however, that her place would be filled sometime by somebody."

"If ye could make up your mind to it," continued the facetiously quivering lips of the captain's lady, "I should be very glad for Helen to have ye for a mother-in-law. The man's going to harness up Eulalie," she added, in a matter-of-fact tone, "to take ye home."

Margaret gave an involuntary plaintive shriek. "Oh, I beg of you!" she added, with ardor; "I need the exercise. Let me walk home. I am going to walk home along the beach."

"I've heard it's fashionable," said Mrs. Herkimer, "to scrabble along over them tormentin' shore-pebbles and salt-water soak your shoes, but folks here don't do it; but if you're set on it, I'll countermand my orders. Come to-morrow, as early as ye can. I hope ye won't find me in depression."

As she was going out Margaret passed

through the parlor where Helen sat at the piano. " Yesterday," she was singing sadly —"yesterday I wandered in the paths of sin. Yesterday I—"

" Dear little girl," said Margaret, stooping an instant over her, " you never wandered in the paths of sin in your life !"

Helen raised her eyes half doubtfully, as if to something irreligiously attractive.

Margaret—after a "good-night" hug given to Stack, who came and asked her for it— went down the lane again to the beach, strong in the salubrious wind, and thinking how the great shadows of her life seemed to have melted before her and given her a place.

Enraptured with the sunset, she took the stroll at her own leisure, until, about half the distance covered, she caught a glimpse of two figures sitting together on a natural shelf in a cave of the cliffs, well retired. It was Mildred St. Thomas's brilliant parasol, obvious, though furled ; and the other, if she had known it, was the burly form of Jeffrey Sprague.

"Mildred has chosen a romantic place to chat with some admirer," thought Margaret, passing, still leisurely, with her face to the sea, as though she had not seen. No other sign of humanity greeted her till she had climbed the rocky path and gained the street; there, astride the nearest lamp-post, with his legs encircling the cage at the top, sat Plantagenet Stuart. Thinking he too might be enjoying stolen sweets as a fugitive from home, Margaret passed on obliviously.

"Ahem! Ahem!" said the arresting voice of Plantagenet, much embarrassed. It was now distinctly revealed by the rays of the lamp that he had a new cap on, and on its fore-piece blazed the letters, "H.M.S. *Mohawk*."

When he perceived that Margaret's eyes had discerned so much, he lifted the cap, as it were, incidentally, careful, however, to keep its blood-curdling legend in the foreground.

"What a beautiful new cap you have, Plantagenet."

Blush after blush of uncontainable pride surged through the grime of his features; the near contact of the light made celestial glory of his tawny, untracked mop of hair; his face gave suggestions through the dirt of some wild flower going and blowing its own glad way in the wilderness.

Margaret regarded his potential beauty with a sort of pensive pang at the heart, and went on; presently she heard footsteps following.

"Say! Would ye like to take my book on *Kings and Quanes?*"

"Why, yes, dear; but don't you need it at school?"

"Pooh! 'tain't a school-book, it's *interest-in*'. Mar giv' it to me one Chris'mas; it's on our fam'ly—ourn and yourn."

"Why, yes, in that case, I must read it, surely. Bring it up to my room some time, dear."

"'Tain't proper, is it," said Plantagenet, straightening himself to the utmost of his sturdy twelve years, "for a *gen'leman* to come up to your room—is it?"

"Don't lecture me on propriety, my little lad," said Margaret, laughing. "It's quite proper for a little boy like you to come up to my room, if I do you the honor to ask you, but not to kick the key out of the door for introduction, as you did when you first showed me the way!"

"Gee!" said the proud one, gasping, "you're like her!"

"Like whom?"

"Quane Sen' Marie Stuart. I tell ye she was an eagle, she was! She could ride hoss-back ninety-six miles to a stretch. Oh, she could spit, she could! If I'd been a-livin', what happened to her ud never 'a' happened. I'd 'a' brought out the Pluck and Liver Kore!"

"Oh, Plantagenet, what is the 'Pluck and Liver' Corps?"

"It's my mil't'ry comp'ny."

He procured the book and brought it up to her door, "H.M.S. *Mohawk*" still pointedly displayed in his hand.

The book was an excessively worn tradition of the era of Mary Stuart, so partisan

in political and religious tendencies as almost to burn the covers; and as for its physical qualities, they were so strongly evident
that every leaf seemed, like Mrs. O'Ragan's
brown beef, to be "dressed with an onion."

Margaret put it outside a window, under
shield of the blind, there permanently to air
until such time as it should be courteous to
return it.

## CHAPTER V

A DAY or two after this, as Margaret was doing some shopping in the town, she heard a voice of indignation and menace :

"You *stole* dat cap! You stole it out my show-box!"

A slighter and gentler Jew laid his hand on the angry vender's arm. "Well, if he did, nevertheless you are to let him go," said Isaac Gilchrist, in a tone of authority; and, for some reason, the wrathful one instantly relaxed his hold.

"There! You old 'Scariot Bologny Sausage, you!" cried the accused Plantagenet, triumphantly.

"Come here, Pleg!" said the liberator, in a gentle and familiar way.

But without distinction in the Israelitish camp, Pleg took to his heels.

"Did he steal the cap?" said Margaret.

"I'm afraid so." Isaac lifted his hat with
a pleasant smile of greeting. "Ah, he's a
wild boy, and if I can keep the hand of the
law off of him to some good account in the
end, I shall have solved *one* mystery," he
said, quite merrily for him, and walking on
with her apace through the busy street.
"And how is it with you? Are you getting
used to us? Are you well? Are you happy?"

"Oh yes, I am at work and doing nicely,
thank you. And do you go about," she
said, after a pause, demurely, "delivering
naughty boys out of their prospective dun-
geons?"

"I? Ah, no. I am a lazy man. I read
very much in my room. I have written and
published some things, but on the whole I
am too perplexed to write much."

His coarse but immaculate clothes and
fine linen; his quiet, unconscious manner of
authority piqued Margaret with a sense of
curiosity and interest. But he went on, in
his matter-of-fact tone:

"I am the son of a Jew who started in
business here in a small way; later, as his

means increased, he employed a tutor and
sent me abroad. I was an only child, and
he and my mother are both dead. I am not
poor. I own the shop where our little friend
appropriated his cap — and other shops. I
suppose I might build myself a house of
some pretensions, but I do not seem to care
for it. I am rather studying—many things."

"If you are studying humanity and its
philosophies and religions and come to any
conclusion, do let me know," said Margaret,
rather too cheerfully to inflict him with any
flattering sense of appreciation.

"Oh, I would do so," he replied, with the
utmost seriousness; "and meantime I wish
you to understand," he continued, in his
perfectly unemotional manner, "that you
are to rely upon me; you are to come to me
if there is any trouble you do not know how
to bear."

"Why?" The incredulous color mounted
to her face and a flash to her laughing eyes.

"'Why?'—even in the Old Book we are
told, as we are placed, to be kind to one
another, are we not?"

"I think we have rather grown to adapt that, both in the Old Book and the New, to our own articles of convenience," she said, with a pleasant satire she could not resist.

A look of pain came over his face. "That is one of my perplexities," he said.

They were nearing the house together, and instead of suffering any sense of annoyance therefor, something of his own impersonal seriousness so impressed Margaret that his company seemed rather to confer a protective distinction upon her.

She held out her hand to him. "I did not mean to be flippant. What you say is true; but I think a sort of hopelessness, in great things, has come over us; at least, when one dreads hard things as I do," she added, with her bright smile, "the exigencies of every-day existence are about as much as we can contend with."

He looked at her kindly, with his foreign, almost prophetic, eyes, and she left him, not without a sense of relief, the groundwork of her nature being substantially joyous. So, when she looked out of her front window and saw Plantagenet, under maledictions from an upper-story oracle, sniffing voluptuously at some parcels he was assisting the grocer's boy to deliver, her heart warmed towards him.

"Stop smellin' the issence out o' my truck, ye little tormint, Pleg Stuart, or I'll be down on ye!" cried the voice; at which Plantagenet drew so long and loud a sniff at a package of coffee that, but for the interruption caused by his own excessive laughter, it seemed likely to burst its cerements. So unmixed a note of joy Margaret had never heard, so free from any self-conscious tremor even under reprobation.

The window above went down with a bang, indicating that footsteps were about to follow.

"Plantagenet!" called Margaret, softly. "Come, there's something in your book I want you to explain to me." Almost before she could finish speaking she heard the bound of his bare feet on the backstairs. She let him in and closed the door.

"Now here," she said, careful to take

the book of glorious ancestry in her gloved
hands, and turning the pages with a quick
intention of finding the thing she wished.
"Ah, here," indicating the text with a lilac
kid finger. "'They might be exterminated,
but they could not be conquered.' Now, of
course, with such a spirit as that, they—they
could not *steal*, could they, Plantagenet?"

"Oh yes, they did!" cried the descendant
of kings, with eager information. "They all
stoled—ships, and jew'ls, and money, and—"

"But Mary Stuart, you know—*our* family
—she did not steal!"

"N—n—o, she didn't steal."

"Well, we don't mind the rest, we want
to be like *our* family. Now I want you to
go and take back the cap, and tell the man
you are sorry for what you said to him."

"Well, I ain't goin' to."

Margaret had worked around to the door,
and she stood with her back against it; she
was tall and vigorous, but Plantagenet too
had the soul of the Stuarts.

"I tell ye, I ain't goin' to."

His beautiful deep eyes seemed to affirm

their purpose through a perpetual hunger, madly joyful though enshadowed, like Margaret's own. But the woman had the longer experience in having her own way, with natural devices unknown to the ragged little reprobate who confronted her: he seemed so like herself; besides, with honest pity of him, the tears came to her eyes.

" Well, b' darn, I'll go!" said he, like a gentleman.

" Then go and do it *quick*," said Margaret, gladly yielding him the door; "go the way 'our family' do when they're out—conquering; go like Mary, at the rate of ninety-six miles an hour !"

She followed at a distance, to purchase " H.M.S. *Mohawk* " as soon as it had been restored to the legitimate channels of trade, and came home with that identical cap in a neat parcel under her arm.

Plantagenet, who was drilling his corps in the front yard, looked up at her with his hungry, merry eyes from under the ragged unemblematized head-piece that now formed his flower of tournament.

The lilac finger beckoned him aside.

"Did you go, dear?"

"Yes'm."

"And gave up the cap, and said you were sorry?"

"No!" said Plantagenet, too proud of the fact to lie in this instance; "I thrun it at him!"

Margaret sighed, not without perceptible satisfaction. With polite formalities of concession, she realized the true Stuart sense of not admitting one's self in the wrong, or apologizing, therefore, to human soul. So she produced the cap, a full consciousness of Plantagenet's atonement glowing on her charming face. "It has been bought. It is your very own, now, dear."

He looked at it, then at her, and with one lionlike bound threw his arms around her neck and smacked her forcibly and loudly on the cheek. Realizing his affront, humiliation replaced his ardor with painful blushes. "I tell ye what it is," said he, sheepishly, "I'm soft on you!"

Margaret went up the stairs laughing.

Mrs. O'Ragan took advantage of this witness to say proudly to Mrs. Shaughnessy : "Did it annoy ye, me dressin' me breakfast wid onions this mornin', Mrs. Shaughnessy, ma'am ? I persaved the odor wint through the house."

"Not at all, Mrs. O'Ragan," replied the other, with an equal blandishment of society grace. " Faith, I wish I had a half-dizzen of the same on a plate afore me this instant."

"Poor cratur!" Margaret heard, as she closed her door; " to my certain knowledge, she 'ain't had a cabbage bilin' senct she came here. Begorry, I sh'd have sech a cabbage thirst on me there'd be no holdin' me off. I'd offer her a bit, only these Bamboos bes so quare."

"Thrue for ye. Mrs. Soollivan tells me the Jew that takes his males wid her niver thanks God by atin' the hid of a cabbage, espicially if there's an ilegant bit o' pork biled in wid it."

" All the same, he's a good young man— the holy saints convart them both ! But hould the lady to me for a Bamboo, though

6

she has me own name, wid a washin' out every evenin', like she was playin' dolls."

But it was no play to Margaret. Composedly changing her raiment as often as had ever been her wont, and as though such extreme fastidiousness were an inflexible law of nature, she was dismayed to find that when she was not consoling Mrs. Herkimer at seven cents an hour she was bound and wedded to the exigencies of her own wash-tub, at first with bitter tears of weariness and vexation, but now evermore with growing stoicism, especially as the tenement clothes-line was weak and her toil had often to be duplicated. Her familiar figure in the yard, stringing her immaculate clothing along the line in unskilled fashion and with gloved hands, provoked the gleeful comment of the tenement.

"'Tis a stiddy washer ye are, Mrs. Stuart," said Mrs. O'Ragan, whistling through the clothes-pins she held in her mouth, and who had made a feint of hanging out a dish-towel in order to be nearer the present source of enlivenment.

"Yes," said Margaret, gravely and unsuspiciously, "I wash very steadily."

"'Tis many a poor widdy," continued Mrs. O'Ragan, tentatively, "gets no insurance on her man whin he dies. But, I praise God, when O'Ragan Stuart goes, he'll be doin' me wan good turn onyway. Faith, if such a sad evint should happen, and me able to survive the grafe, I'd be better off and aisier livin' by far, Mrs. Stuart, than ye see me livin' this day!"

Margaret paused in listening wonder, with the sleeve of a lace-enshrouded night-robe suspended in air.

"Sure, yes," continued Mrs. O'Ragan, delighted with her audience and forgetting the facetiousness of Margaret's performance in the delectable enterprise of her own imagination; "'tis better off I'd be."

"But if you are fond of him and would feel the loss so, I do not see how—"

"Oh, begorry, Mrs. Stuart, ma'am! Well, thin, ''tis a wise cow that carries short horns.'" With which utterance she tightened her waist-cable and departed.

"Hang it not so," said a new voice, and a
voice Margaret liked to hear—"hang it not
by de sleeve, it shall blow itself a rent.  I
shall show you!  I seen you," continued
Agnes, her comely face shining—"I seen
you wid my dear young mans."

"*Is* he young?" said Margaret, wearily.

"You are tired, you are discusted wid so
much wash."  Agnes put her young, motherly arm around her.  "Come to my rooms,
now, soon it is evenin', and we shall play
you 'armony."

Margaret had ignored Agnes with the rest
of the tenement, socially, and now, depressed
and tired, she had a fancy for complying.

When she came, Agnes received her as
though she were quite in the habit of spend-
ing her evenings there.  Mr. Sullivan rose and
shook hands heartily, then retired with ex-
clusive seriousness to his newspaper.

"Oh, this is good, to find you here!" said
Isaac Gilchrist when he entered.  "I have
been very anxious about you to-day."  His
dark eyes rested on her a moment in their
peculiar, tender, impersonal way.  In her

present mood this undeserved and uncalled-
for regard was grateful to Margaret. From
the confidence his presence inspired she gave
him, unconsciously, in her weariness, a look
instinctively large, with despair and gratitude almost childishly mingled. A light
swept over his dispassionate face.

Two of Plantagenet's "Pluck and Liver
Corps" — Agnes's youngest, mere tin-pan
players—were partitioned off by a graceful
curtain in a section of the drawing-room,
there supposed to be slumbering on their
cot after the conflicts of the day. But Margaret, who had an instinctive affiliation with
small boys, saw four beautiful brown eyes
peering through a convenient opening in the
draperies while Isaac swept the strings of
his violin.

Conscious finally of this mutual regard, the
boys revealed their pleasure by a giggle.

"Roy! 'Onry!" said Agnes, lovingly.

"My toof aches, mamma."

Agnes went to the cot and took up the
complainant, and returned to her chair with
him snuggled in her arms.

The other night-robed figure trotted across the room to his father, who received him and continued reading the newspaper over him.

It was a scene so full of homely peace and affection, Margaret's own heart sank to rest —when Mrs. O'Ragan summoned her at the door.

"Is Mrs. Stuart widin? 'Tis Miss Duds Sen' Tammy is callin', and says, could she see her the wan moment? She'll only be detainin' her the wan moment."

Margaret found Mildred waiting at her door. " Don't light the lamp," said the girl, as they went in. The moonlight filled the room. " I suppose they're mad at me?"

" Who?"

" The Herkimers."

" Why, no—they always speak very kindly of you!"

" Then you never told them you saw me sitting down by the shore with Jeff? I thought you wouldn't."

"Oh, was that Jeff? I did not notice; I did not know."

"Oh, I tell you, it's rocky!" said Mildred,

her voice quivering, almost breaking, with tears. "We do love each other, Jeff and me. It's just plain—through quarrels and everything else we come back to it. It's just like we had a little kitchen together, all warm, and the lamp lit, and the table set. Jeff's plain—his mother was a working girl; and anyway it's me Jeff's wants; it ain't Helen Herkimer."

"I can hardly blame him!"

"Then you don't think I ought to give him up?" said Mildred, eagerly. "We can go away together and work — he's willing enough."

Margaret had never given up any one she loved except by the inexorable law of death.

"Is Helen *very* fond of him, do you fancy?"

"Oh, she—she—just worships him, the way that kind does wild boys."

"Mildred, dear, I don't know what to say. I— Ask Agnes," was on her lips to say. Isaac Gilchrist's face, set calmly, without even the shadow of conscious self-abnegation amid the stormy passions of life, rose before her. "But for Helen's sake this must not be known. Perhaps it will all come right. Be patient—wait—"

Mildred hid her face by the bed in a storm of sobs.

"It *won't* come right, I know well enough. You say there's a good God; then why did He put us here just to worry us and torment us?"

It was a question not unknown to Margaret in desperate hours, with set lips silently. It rushed upon her now, and she hid her face beside the girl's.

"I don't know. I don't know why, in one way and another, He takes away the good, sweet things we love, and leaves us in the cold and dark, desolate. But even so, I must love or I shall die! And I love *you*, Mildred. It isn't like his young, dear love, I know, but oh, I love you! And the question you have asked is all too ready to come to me. Don't let it make shipwreck of us —help me, Mildred! help me!"

The girl was used to self-sacrifice, the woman quivered at the touch of pain.

The grave look of self-control came back to Mildred's tear-stained face. "I'm wicked and cruel to bring such troubles of mine to you."

"No, you would be cruel *not* to come. Will you remember that? for it is true. Promise me to remember in this or any trouble, you are cruel *not* to come." Her strong, slender fingers grasped the girl's hard hand.

"I can't see that — I can't see anything much; but I feel somehow like a taut line just draws me here when I'm rocky—and I'm all right now."

"Oh, the poor, poor girl!" moaned Margaret when she was gone. "If we could all only be like Isaac Gilchrist — loveless, humanitarian, emotionless, studying life, not drowned in it!" Again his dark eyes seemed to dwell upon her face—"'I have been very anxious about you to-day.'" Margaret bit her lip in the silence and smiled. "He seemed to know—the old young Hebrew— that I was away down, down in the marshlands of 'Despond' to-day; he seemed to *know* that I do not very well know how to live; he seemed actually to *know* that I have just a dollar and seventy cents in this wide world! I must go early to-morrow and comfort Mrs. Herkimer, and make a bit of money."

## CHAPTER VI

Mrs. Herkimer was standing at the gate with a spy-glass.

At first Margaret was flattered to think it was bearing directly upon her, in anxiety for her approach; but her patroness only said, in an agitated voice, " Have you seen Eulalie?"

" I trust not!" said Margaret, firmly. " All the horses in town not happening to be in harness at this particular time, are feeding along the highway as usual, but I am thankful to say I did not see Eulalie."

Mrs. Herkimer's mouth twitched. " I no sooner see you than I begin to get chirked up. Captain's been off lookin' for her this hour. Our young minister's sick, and I feel called to go and see him, and I want you to accompany me, but it's too far to walk. If it wasn't for the responsibility of money I could wish that Helen had chosen him instead of that wild Jeff." A hope for Mildred sprang in Margaret's heart. "But," continued Mrs. Herkimer, emphatically, "money is a great responsibility; and besides, as a husband, Helen can't abide the thought of him. She's like all the rest of us—she's fixed her heart where perhaps she ain't likely to get consoled."

She sighed significantly, fixing her spyglass on the captain, returning from unsuccessful search, in the distance.

Stack, whom Margaret had meanwhile caressed with that special fondness which prevailed between the two, now tugged at her skirts.

"Go see what he wants," said Mrs. Herkimer, solemnly. "Stack always means something when he does that."

Margaret followed. In behind Mrs. Herkimer's rose-tree at the south wing Stack revealed and disclosed Eulalie nibbling at those precious blossoms, and leaning, for greater security, against the side of the house.

"Oh, you naughty, naughty Eulalie!"

cried Mrs. Herkimer, with dignified reproach.

The captain, now appearing, sprang in and caught her.

" I'm sorry you found her, Stack, dear old fellow!" said Margaret, while she was being harnessed. " Oh, Stack, you would not have found her if you knew how I hate to drive her !"

"I know !" said Stack. "I guess I know! But you are trying to please, and you must do the best you can—the best you can."

" I've discovered this left rein's kinder weak," said the captain, cheerfully, as they climbed in ; "don't twitch up on her there."

As Eulalie's special crime was hard-bittedness, the prospect was more than ever encouraging. But Stack watched them off with benign wistfulness. Invariably with them on the water, he was obedient in not following the highway enterprises of Mrs. Herkimer's chariot; the frightened ejaculations of the women at his size, the whistling away and scattering of mongrel dogs, the awesome and ever-retreating gaze of the small boys, all greatly deterred him with the unmerited pangs of an honest heart.

Meanwhile Eulalie, inflated with her feast of roses, shot forth at her own ugly, spasmodic, ranting pace.

" You like her better, now you're getting to know her, don't you ?" said the captain's lady, seriously.

" No," said Margaret ; " I consider that remark only the fateful acceptance of an apothegm. She inspires me continually with ever-deeper forebodings of calamity and disaster."

Mrs. Herkimer laughed. " Don't you notice," she said, " that she never breaks ?"

" A break from her present gait, whatever it might be, would be agreeable."

The phaetons of Yarmouth, like its lifeboats, were constructed to contend with any sea; so, a wide berth being given them, they rattled on, broad in the beam and mighty in the hub, to their destination.

" Will you come in with me ?"

The view was fine, and—" No," said Margaret, " I would rather stay here."

"If the little crazy house-keeper comes out, you mustn't mind. She's as innocent as harmless, and she's a remarkable cook."

In view of a tête-à-tête with a lunatic, Margaret stepped out and cabled Eulalie to the post. She had but regained her seat when a sprightly little old figure came flying down the path and sprang up beside her.

"I've been waiting for *you!*" she cried, embracing her eagerly. "I knew you'd come! Oh, I knew you'd come!"

"Yes," said Margaret, kindly, "I have come."

A new thought came to the airy brain. She tripped into the house and reappeared with a steaming cup of tea. Again she vanished and returned with cakes and jelly.

"Now, no more, dear," said Margaret; "if you love me, and have been waiting for me so long, you do not wish to make me ill, do you?"

"No, no!" said the other, "we mustn't make *you* ill!" and she leaned her head lightly and contentedly on Margaret's shoulder while the latter tasted the food.

"Why, Zely!" said Mrs. Herkimer, when she came, "have you found such a friend?"

"I've been *waiting* for her," said Zely, and she chatted on mercurially with the captain's lady without the least demonstration of affection towards her.

"I only thought she'd rattle on to you," said Mrs. Herkimer afterwards. "I didn't know she was going to hug ye. She don't do that, as I know of. She must 'a' had a queer kind of a takin' to ye."

"Cranks and imbeciles and lunatics always have," said Margaret, biting her lip.

"Well, now," said Mrs. Herkimer, as soon as she could recover from the facetious aspect of this idea, "I am neither one, and I was strongly attached to ye from the first. Turn to the left."

They drove over a road unexampled for wild beauty, into the driveway of a private park, and confronted an imposing mansion.

"Whose place is this?" said Margaret, wondering.

"I am going to call," said Mrs. Herkimer, "on Judson Sprague's sister, who is keeping house for him now. This is Judson's home."

"I will sit here and hold the horse," said Margaret, rather shortly.

"If you do, Judson will come out and visit with ye. I don't say that he'll offer to hug and kiss ye as Zely did, but he'll be fool enough to want to. Ye'll feel more comfortable to come in."

Margaret's eyes flashed, but she shut her lips under the stress of existence at seven cents an hour; and at this juncture the burly form and rugged, genial features of Jeff appeared.

"Let me fasten the horse."

"I will show you how to tie her," said Margaret, as Mrs. Herkimer sailed off grandly towards the house.

"Oh, I know! I know Eulalie," said Jeff, showing his big white teeth. "I'm rather a special friend down at the Herkimers, you know;" but he gave the latter clause with little animation.

"Alas! I know more about you than you think, my young friend," thought Margaret.

7

But she liked Jeff. They tied Eulalie in the shade and went in together—Margaret suffering an effusive greeting from the elder Sprague at the door—to the cloistered splendors of one of the great parlors.

"I hope you will find a comfortable chair, Mrs. Stuart," said the sister, with solemnity, as if to emphasize further the luxurious upholstery displayed in the room.

Margaret sat down a little apart with Jeff. A boyish desire to make her happy irradiated his plain face, he reached out and took a photograph album, pointing out his family relations to her, at first with dry statistics as to residence and order of propinquity, but gradually working into a vein of great humor and freedom, with running comments hard to resist.

The felicities of one volume exhausted, he reached out for another.

"Jeff," said his father, "have you been to the post?"

"No, sir." Jeff's honest jaw drooped.

"Will you go, my son?"

"Certainly, sir."

The elder Sprague came over and took the chair thus perfunctorily vacated.

"After the cruel impression you left upon me, both the first and last time we ever met, Mrs. Stuart, how has Mrs. Herkimer persuaded you to visit my humble home?"

"I came merely as Mrs. Herkimer's companion."

"Ah, too bad! too bad! But allow me to say the companion outshines the matron, to my eyes, as the sun the moon."

"Very much obliged, I'm sure," said Margaret, dryly. "You have exceedingly charming views here."

"You will be surprised perhaps that on an estate of this size I keep only three servants—a man for the garden, and two maids in the house. It is my great desire, if I could find a sufficient incentive—ah, a companion who would encourage me—to extend the style of my house-keeping on a more sumptuous and hospitable scale."

Mrs. Herkimer and the sister, according to the custom of old seaport towns, had turned their backs upon this eligible pair and become deeply engrossed in conversation. Margaret, with anger in her heart, thus basely deserted to mischief, determined to make the most of the precarious advantage.

"Your sister seems to be a most amiable companion," she said.

"Ah, too bad! too bad! Have the ties of the past been so precious to you, Mrs. Stuart, that you could not even contemplate forming new ones for the future?"

"Possibly — but that would depend altogether upon circumstances."

"Then I am going to hope your circumstances may become more and more reduced!"

"You misunderstand me. There is no combination of circumstances that could drive me to take a step I did not wish to take."

"Ah, how you would shine in a generous establishment! Too bad! too bad! But if one comes only as a slave at your feet?"

"I have no desire for slaves. Mrs. Herkimer, Eulalie is such an unreliable beast, do

not you think we would better be making
some investigations as to what her present
misconduct may be?"

"Patrick has put her in the barn," said
the sister, in her solemn voice. "We shall
lay it up as a slight if you do not both stay
to luncheon."

Mrs. Herkimer, who had evidently already
composed herself to this idea, did not dare
look at Margaret. They were about to re-
sume their conversation.

"I do not like to have you turn your
backs on me," said Margaret, simply.

The sister looked with considerable surprise at one who attempted such innovations
on the established framework of society.

"You must come up to the blue-room and
take off your things," she said, when she had
recovered her breath.

Mrs. Herkimer kept close to her, not wishing any confidential communion with Margaret at this time.

But when, having reached this bourn, they
looked out of the windows and saw it rain-
ing, the captain's lady resumed her mantle

of superior dignity. "Well, it's fortunate we accepted!" she said. "The shower will probably be over by the time we wish to go."

"We have ample guest-rooms," said the sister, with a sad, proud smile, as though such a self-evident fact should hardly have been brought to the exigency of comment.

Margaret got near Mrs. Herkimer. "If you stay overnight, I shall walk home," she whispered.

"I have no intention of staying overnight!" said Mrs. Herkimer, in her recovered state, quite reprovingly.

The luncheon-table was so loaded with silver and cut-glass the sense was oppressive. Poor Jeff spilled his glass of claret on the damask cloth and dropped his fork twice, but even in the midst of such discouragements kept his ingenuous smile of good-fellowship directed at Margaret across the table.

"Ah, too bad! Aren't you a bit clumsy to-day, my son?"

"I'm always clumsy, father."

The elder Sprague wished Margaret's eyes

would rest on him with the frank liking they
gave to this wayward youth.

Remaining, to the very moment, the tech-
nical length of time prescribed by Yarmouth
good-manners after partaking of such glit-
tering hospitality, Mrs. Herkimer finally rose
and announced her intention of going.

Jeff was sent to tell Patrick to harness
Eulalie; he came springing back, his white
teeth gleaming and a good-natured laugh in
his eyes.

"Oh, Mrs. Herkimer, you're going home
with the drollest, prettiest little colt!"

"Haven't you anything better to do, Jeffrey," said Mrs. Herkimer, with motherly for-
bearance, "than to make fun of poor Eulalie? There are many older horses, though
I know Eulalie is no colt!"

"But she's — she's *got* a colt, Mrs. Herkimer — such a droll little thing, running all
about!"

Confirmation of this appalling statement
was now afforded by the spectacle of Patrick
leading Eulalie down the driveway, the colt
— all legs — making this condign occasion

more lamentable by his unappreciative frisk-
iness.

Mrs. Herkimer compressed her lips. Never
had Margaret seen such solemnity on her
features as when she shook hands with her
entertainers, uttering the usual common-
places of farewell.

Jeff was opening an umbrella to see Margaret down the path, but his father anticipated him, interposing his own silk canopy
between her and the clouds. So Jeff went
ahead, sheltering Mrs. Herkimer.

Margaret, with her light step and head
well carried, chatted cheerfully of the prospect of clearing weather, of the extraordi-
nary beauty of the landscape. She dared
not look ahead at the supernal dignity of
Mrs. Herkimer's carriage, nor at other features of the near prospect.

Accustomed to having women duck their
heads nervously under the umbrella and
hold to its progress, the elder Sprague was
now compelled rather to dance a watchful
attendance upon his companion, so erect
and indifferently she sailed on.

"This is the woman for my enlarged establishment!" thought he.

"I have a feeling," he murmured, "that you will not always be so inconsiderate of a sincere—adorer."

In the agitation of the moment he knocked her hat with a corner of the umbrella, and saw with dismay the rain-drops falling on her sweet face.

She smiled, untroubled and unvexed. "Treasure that feeling," she drawled, coolly, as if with a subtle suggestion there might be less warrant for it in the future.

The two women drove on silently until, at a discreet distance from the house, the colt forsook its mother for some wayside investigations and Eulalie stopped short with a watchful sideways cast of body; then Margaret handed the lines to Mrs. Herkimer and shrieked with laughter. The captain's lady waited quietly.

"When you get through," said she, "I'll take my turn."

"This must be done now," she said, "and forever afterwards repressed. My inmost

feelings are far otherwise from mirthful. I
was not informed. The captain knew what
was likely to happen. I—I am almost inclined," she said, in a deep voice, "to visit
him with corporeal punishment!"

"I will assist you with all my heart," said
Margaret.

The captain himself, when he saw them
approaching—the colt having by this time
got down to a steady stalking gait, the
weather now quite clear and a fresh wind
blowing — looked at first with a searching
intentness, then, as the truth burst upon him,
turned his head in a sort of sickly despair,
and as they drew nearer even affected to
whistle.

"Well," said Mrs. Herkimer, "here we
are!"

The tone implied bodily attack, and Margaret only waited the initiative from her
protectress.

"The tide serves and the moon's full!"
said the captain, turning his guilty face towards them. "We must have a sail this evening!"

It was the one point on which he could ever hope to begin to be restored to the favor of his lady. The serving of the tide and a sail were ever as manna to her soul, but she did not yield so readily—not she.

"What do you think of yourself, Captain Herkimer?"

"I hadn't no idea it was goin' to happen so soon —on my word, I hadn't, Nell!" he protested, but his face broke into a fateful grin at the antics of his new and untoward possession.

"Smile—smile if you can, Captain Herkimer! I shall never hold my head up again!" Having said this, and holding her head very high indeed, Mrs. Herkimer swept into the house. "You must stay to-night, Mrs. Stuart. I can never live through the night without the consciousness that you are under my roof."

"Yes, I will stay." It came to Margaret that she might chance upon a little private conversation with Helen, and learn, in a casual way, the stringency of her affection for Jeff, in whom, for Mildred's sake, as well as his

own boyish fate, she had become sincerely
interested. "But," she added, referring to
the captain, "shall you forgive him so soon?
It has grown a perfect evening, and, as you
say, the tide serves; but shall you go sailing
this evening?"

"The pangs of remorse," replied Mrs.
Herkimer, "are no less on the ocean than
on the land!" and with an evident intention
that, though bounding joyfully on the ca-
prices of the deep, the captain should not
forget the torments of that never-dying
worm, she meanwhile laid aside her bonnet.

## CHAPTER VII

HELEN looked on with grave disapproval while the captain pulled up an eel-trap or two and emptied the contents into a box.

"What would people think of a man of your professions and money," said his lady, "out here by moonlight, stealin' snakes?"

"Pshaw! I've only took half o' what there was in two traps, and they'll fill up again before morning. 'Snakes!' They're fine eatin'. They're worth a dollar apiece over in the States!"

"Poor souls! Have you got to take pattern after all the heathen that you know of, Captain Herkimer?"

To Margaret, this sail by moonlight along an untamed coast was an ecstasy. The intimation of theft, the wriggling of the eels in the box, only made more weird such lawless riding of the waves; her eyes sparkled

with laughing encouragement at the chief
marauder, the captain, while Helen, near to
whom she sat, steered sadly, watching the
self-abandoned sympathy with the elements
on the older woman's face.

"What should you do if something should
happen to the boat, Mrs. Stuart — if there
should be danger?" she said, wistfully.

"I feel as though I should hardly care,"
laughed Margaret. "If we were riding so
fast, and a wind like this, I know I should
not drown, I should go *somewhere* nice!"

"What church *do* you belong to?"

"Oh, the Presbyterian; but at heart, I
fear, always a wretched little Catholic, of
the old days, when they could not read
and a few images were enough!" Margaret spoke, with laughing half earnestness,
in a low voice, but Helen shuddered. "My
dear little girl," the Stuart went on, "every
thought is so hackneyed, so attenuated,
in these days, the brain has outgrown the
limbs that carry it and is a deformity.
There is this theory and that theory, and
lots of pale people in spectacles running to

hear them expounded. I envy the brown and red fish-wife, with a shawl over her head and no alphabet, who gets down by a way-side cross and tells her beads. We theorize, she *sees ;* we hardly hope, she *knows.*"

The girl listened, fascinated, but too chary even to attempt comprehension.

At this point something slimy and ser-pentine began to wind itself round Marga-ret's ankle. She gave a shriek as impetuous and clearly defined as the edge of a knife, and sprang, still shrieking, into Helen's arms.

The captain rushed over and captured a large eel which had escaped consignment to the box by oversight; he also took the helm while Helen held Margaret.

"It was only an eel, Mrs. Stuart; dear Mrs. Stuart, father has put it in the box; it was only an eel." At which Margaret only emitted another piercing scream.

The captain left the helm momentarily, and, lifting the box, precipitated its entire contents into the water. The sound of the struggling and writhing ceased.

"They're all back in the water, Mrs. Stuart. Father has emptied them all into the water."

Margaret first grew cold, then trembled, then sobbed, then laughed again. The grave Helen got the impression that she was a spirit possibly much subject to "mad fits" in her childhood, and that her usual commendable self-control was perhaps primarily a matter of culture rather than of native predilection.

"I never had a snake *near* me before," said the Stuart, relapsing into Mrs. Herkimer's own terms. "In Fox's *Book of Martyrs*, when my old nurse used to read me about putting people into bags of them, I always had to scream. It isn't a matter of courage; I'd rather die. I've always known I never could bear *that!*" She glanced with dilated eyes about the boat.

"They're every one of 'em overboard," said Mrs. Herkimer in a soothing voice. "You see now," she said, with the utmost solemnity to the captain, "what's come o' your didos with them eels." The poor captain steered on, deeply oppressed by this culminating disaster of the day.

"Oh, do get some more, captain, if you wish!" cried Margaret. "I could look out another time; it was being taken so by surprise. Still, if you don't mind going without—"

"There's not going to be any more eel tantrums in this boat!" said Mrs. Herkimer, decidedly.

"Anybody'd think I did it a-purpose!" exclaimed the captain. "I wouldn't 'a' had it happen for anything."

"When we set out by breaking the commandments—" began his lady.

"Breaking your granny!" cried the captain, desperate in his woe, and would hear no more.

"We will have devotions to-night," said Mrs. Herkimer, with meaning, when they reached home.

Helen set a lamp on the piano.

"Will you read, or shall I, Captain Herkimer? Helen will then sing."

The captain, who was too manly to continue pettish, took the Bible reverently and turned to the fluid sentences of a reassuring psalm.

"We must remember," said Mrs. Herkimer at the close, "that *those* promises are for such as keep the narrow way. Will you sing, Helen, ' Yesterday I wandered ' ?"

"' Yesterday I wandered in the paths of sin.'"

Helen's sweet spirit-burdened voice filled the room with an uneasy awe.

The Stuart, nervous as only a high-strung animal can be at some slimy incident, still casting an occasional involuntary glance along the floor, met the captain's generally cool and contemptuous bearing with a wide, startled smile of sympathy in her eyes.

"P'sh !" said the hero of many seas at the close of these exercises.  " Anybody 'd think I was lost just because I took a dozen of Ed Harris's eels, when he's told me a thousand times to help myself."

"It's the spirit and not the letter," said Mrs. Herkimer, finally.

" What we need is a good night's rest,"

said the sea-veteran, cheerfully. "We ain't got half a dozen brains between us as it is."

"A good conscience is better than a mountain of the brilliantest brains," said his lady.

"It may be better," replied the captain, " but conscience without brains makes a devilish poor show."

His disappearance with these words was timely and instantaneous.

Helen accompanied Margaret to her room.

" You must not be nervous to-night," said the girl, setting down the lamp. " After all, it was nothing, you know."

"Oh, I shall not be nervous!" said Margaret, quite with her usual manner. " But what a charming fire! I love a climate where one can always enjoy a fire at night. Sit down a moment, dear!"

Helen sat down not far from the enigma, and watched her composed face and retrospective eyes kindling in the firelight.

Margaret did not hurry. "Should you have acted as I did about that *eel?*" she asked, at last, tranquilly.

Helen, too, took time for thought. "No," she said, very gravely.

"But why not? Are you used to being embraced by—creeping things?"

"No, I am not used to them."

"Well, then, Helen, why not?"

"Because I try to be always prepared for hard things—any hard thing."

"Oh, my child," said Margaret, impetuously, "you ought not to feel that way—so good and so young, and with such a happy future before you!" But her heart smote her at that last clause. Perhaps Helen was wise, after all.

"I do not know that my future will be happy."

"But you are engaged"—Margaret spoke in a tentatively delicate way—"to such a nice young man. I met him to-day. I think he is a dear boy."

"He is dear enough," said the girl, shyly, and her lips trembled.

"This poor child is like the sea she was born by," thought Margaret, "deep and *sad*. Mildred should give him up—yes, Mildred should give him up. But he *loves* Mildred!"

The girl, watching her enigma's face, saw it perplexed and wearily saddening in the firelight, and, without knowing the cause, her heart was moved to a sudden confidence.

"Yes, he is dear enough, Mrs. Stuart; so dear that I could myself endure to suffer or be deprived of anything if it was for his happiness and good. I *know* that."        .

In her self-contained life this impulse to confession shook her almost as if it had been a crime.

"Let us hope for *happy* things — *happy* things," said Margaret, rising in her own bright way. She bent down and kissed the girl; her very presence gave a sense of personal endearment.

Helen's thoughts turned ever rapidly from her own case to care for others. "Now you must not get nervous in a strange room in the night," she repeated. "Remember, it was nothing." She paused a moment, standing. "And remember," she said, as if still under a spell of confession, "if ever you needed me as a friend, if ever there was any hard thing, I would do it for you."

Margaret looked into her dark eyes. Many had said that to her in the sanguine day of prosperity who had tacitly fallen off in adversity.

"I believe you, dear," she said.

"I did not take to her at first," said Margaret, alone, musing over the fire, "because I had thought she had no mitigating sense of humor whatever. Possibly she has something less easily to be spared. Still—it is lugubrious." She shrugged her shoulders, her glance wandering, startled, about the floor again. She heard a soft "tap! tap!" at the door; she opened it, and there stood Stack; he entered and immediately stretched himself on the rug thereby.

"Helen sent you!" cried Margaret, joyfully.

"Anyway, I came," said Stack, closing his august eyes and already pretending to snore.

"But you must eat this cake I saved for you, you dear fellow!" said Margaret, producing the prize from her pocket.

He munched it, adoring her.

"Well, good-night then!" The lace of her sleeve fell over his shaggy neck in a caress.

His steady breathing sent her off to sleep, reassured her in those waking moments which might otherwise have been afflicted with tremors. For uncanny noises disturbed that night. The new puppy broke his chain, and weirdly, wailingly, bayed the moon hour after hour under her window. Eulalie, more than usually indifferent to propriety under the prestige of motherhood, led or followed her colt in ghoulish wanderings and antics about the lawn in the immediate vicinity of the house, kicking tragically at the garden gate, calling shrilly, and shaking the gaunt apple-trees, subsiding into a deceptive silence only to startle the night with some new and hideous vagary of conduct. It seemed at some point in these proceedings that Margaret heard the captain's voice in the big hall below, directed widely, like the general *reveille* of a trumpet:

"Why the —— don't some o' ye get up?

It's half after seven! The girl's had the coffee made an hour!"

Mrs. Herkimer, who had left her hall door open for circulation of air, rose and pointedly shut it to.

Margaret, laughing to herself, sprang out of bed and released Stack, who stood patiently waiting at the door with averted head, and who never once looked at her in her night-robe.

She was in a sunny humor at breakfast, and even Helen seemed to reflect hope from her.

" How many seconds o' sleep did you get last night, Mrs. Stuart?" said Mrs. Herkimer, who had herself been sleepless and felt the necessity for severity.

" Oh, I slept ever so much! I had Stack at the door," and she unreservedly cut out the tenderloin from her steak and laid it one side for a purpose.

" There now, don't, Mrs. Stuart," said the captain, beaming beatifically, " I'll save him some from the dish."

" No," said the Stuart, with childish monopoly of privilege, "I thought of it first. It's my trick!"

"Yarmouth is the only place," persisted Mrs. Herkimer, but without so much asperity as she had shown at first—"the only place I ever was in where puppies and horses were allowed to beset creation all night long with their 'go as you please'!"

"Why, Yarmouth's the only place you ever lived in, anyway, Nell," said her husband.

"I've dwelt weeks at foreign ports," said the lady, majestically, ignoring the interruption.

"Well, yes; but Yarmouth's the only place you ever lived in steady."

"Steady! Do you call it living steady to be hallooed at all night with the didos of wild beasts, and awakened by profanity in the morning?"

Margaret burst fearlessly into laughter; the captain followed with a whole heart. Helen bit her lip and choked. Mrs. Herkimer herself succumbed, finally drying the mirthful tears from her eyes.

"I wish you'd marry into the family," she said, half facetiously, half earnestly, to the Stuart, bidding her good-bye at the door—for Margaret felt the necessity of looking to her affairs at the tenements—"meanin', of course, Judson."

"We will see," said Margaret, who, with health and hope and the ringing air of the morning, felt ready to jest with fate.

And lo! his carriage overtook her as she walked down towards the town.

"Ah, how fortunate, Mrs. Stuart! I am going your way, and my sister is with me, see! Now I beg of you, do me the honor."

He had alighted and was addressing her in a low, unctuous voice.

"I enjoy and need the walk. I really prefer to walk; thank you very much!"

"Ah, too bad! too bad! Still cruel? Well—" The sister looked at her with wondering disapproval—as a vagrant from privilege. He regained his seat, and the rich equipage rolled out of sight.

Margaret walked on, conscious as she neared the town of the mean little rooms

STUART AND BAMBOO 123

awaiting her, which her dainty garments swept incongruously, of an impoverished larder, of a cooking-stove which either bellowed with flame up the chimney or threw out smoke at her, of the merciless, insistent wash-tubs and the halting clothes-line, and she shivered and sighed.

"What is the use, after all, when I might —ugh! But don't ask me too many times" —she laughed softly and insolently after the retreating carriage—" or perhaps, after all, I shall get in and ride with you!"

## CHAPTER VIII

"Plontogonet's gone on progriss, Mrs. Stuart, ma'am."

" On progress !"

" Yes, drat take him! From the book o' *Kings and Quanes* he's got it. And the school-teacher's been sindin' down here to tell me she's never seen the light o' him this day, nor tin others he's beguiled off wid him for a ratinue. Begorry, I'd rat him if I had him betune my two honds !"

Mrs. O'Ragan was in evil spleen. "Pathrick!" she said, with a groan, to a small heir who was not off on progress, "run over to Dr. McGuire and tell him I'm did wid the pain and nade a bit o' midicine. Run now !

" I had a benanny thirst on me this mornin'," she explained to Margaret, "and I squinched it wid a half-dizzen benannys aff a cart, and they lift me groanin'."

The small boy returned. "The doctor says, sind to the sody-water man and git a anterdote."

"How much be they? Here, take a quarther, and if they're expinsive git a small one, and hurry wid ye!"

The boy returned breathless. "The sody man says, what do ye want a anterdote for?"

Mrs. O'Ragan gasped with indignation. "Go offer him yer money, fair," said she, at length, with portentous calm, "and if he don't give ye one, return yerself straight and tell me."

The boy crept back with a haggard air. "He says—he says, what do ye want a anterdote for?"

Mrs. O'Ragan rose, impressively securing her waist-cable; outside she put a shawl of many colors, and a bonnet — evidently the cast-off freak of some fashionable dame. It was extremely small, and Mrs. O'Ragan's head was masterful in proportions; perched, therefore, on the extreme backward summit of her pug of hair, it gave her an aspect so martial that even the heart of a friend shook

at her. Into the bill of a moribund humming-bird which topped the last aspiring
point of this head-piece, dangling, however,
in a tottering position from recent hard
wear, Plantagenet, before he went on progress, had stuffed an entire peanut. But Mrs.
O'Ragan was too excited to observe this
lesser indignity.

As she marched away, awful with over-
perpendicularity of carriage, this sorrowful
bird, at the very summit of her, was the only
thing about her that fluttered, and seemed
trying to disgorge the plebeian fruit which
Plantagenet had all too firmly implanted in
its bill.

"I'll have an antherdote," said she, enter-
ing the drug store with treacherous calm
and displaying a large purse with a gilt
clasp.

"What do you wish an antidote for,
madam?"

"You lay that antherdote down on the
counther and give me the price of it, you
little razor-toed, hair-'iled, rubous-ringed
jude you, or I'll be over behint there and

let you know what I want anything for! I ain't did yit!"

The clerk looked at Mrs. O'Ragan, and hastening to his stores, evolved and tied up with rapid fingers a small parcel which he handed her with unaffected humility.

"Perhaps I could suit you better if I knew what you wished it for, madam, but this is innocuous—"

"Quit now! Quit your langwidge to me!" said Mrs. O'Ragan. "No one ever insoolted me twicet, ye little flea-bite ye! How much is it?"

"A nickel, ma'am."

"What do ye take me fur? Give me a tin-cint one, and make haste wid ye!"

The clerk instantly made substitution of the increased order. And with the contemptuous snort of an easy conqueror, Mrs. O'Ragan, capped by that ennauseated and tottering humming-bird, made her departure.

"Say, mammy," said little Pat, restored in spirit by her successful return with a parcel, "your bird's eatin' a peanut, he is!"

"What bird, thin? What's the child meanin'?"

"The bird in your bunnit's eatin' a peanut, te-he!"

Mrs. O'Ragan divested herself of that proud ornament and found that it was even so.

"Did you know it was fixed on me that shape, thin, whin I wint down to the sody man's?" she said, eying her offspring.

"No, ma'am," said Pat, with instant commendable resource to negation; "I seen it on ye jest as ye was turndin' the cornder home."

"Sure how could ye see it on me behind when I was comin' forninst ye?"

"Why, mammy, I seed ye sideways when ye turndid the cornder! I guess Pleg done it—te-he!—'cause he stoled a peanut off Jimmy las' night."

"I don't guess at all, I know viry will who done it, and when Plontogonet Stuart gets home from this progress, whativer that he's on now, he'll go on another right straight! He'll go on a progress up and down this room wid a sthick after him! That's the nixt progress he'll go on!"

Margaret kept an eye out at her window for the hero's return. She had this unaccountable feeling towards Plantagenet of late, that she would even rather suffer stripes on her own body than have him bear them.

Advanced exploiting parties from the retinue slunk in one by one at dusk—two of Agnes's boys, but she only took them and washed and fed and wept over them for the sorrow they had given her, which they dreaded far more than the beating their comrades looked forward to as the natural corollary of aspiring acts.

At last Margaret saw a sturdy form mounting the cliffs, its garments deplorable, even "II.M.S. *Mohawk*" was rent with the dark significance of some stirring adventure. She caught up a sandwich she had ready prepared and threw a shawl over her head after the manner of the tenements.

Plantagenet expected her, his joyful, hungry eyes glowing larger than ever out of a battle-worn face.

"The 'Pluck and Liver Kore' 's done

9

glorious to day!" said he, devouring the bread and meat in a few gulps.

"I would have brought you more, dear," said Margaret, sitting on a rock at his side, "but it happened to be "—she blushed— "all the meat I had in the house."

"I couldn't eat no more," said the hero, loyally, whose healthy stomach had only been incited to greater desire by the sop offered it.

"I've just made some cake and put it on the iron sink to cool a bit; it will be ready by the time we get down to the house. I've made four loaves!"

The woman's pride was as pathetic as the boy's, and their elated, woe-begone countenances were as if they had been mother and child.

"Oh, you're a giddy house-keeper, you be!" said the commander of the "Pluck and Liver Corps," with tender gallantry. "Say! Sen' Marie Stuart and Botherwell set on a rock jest the same way us is settin', that time they runned away together."

Margaret laughed merrily to the echoes.

A lean kitten came galloping up to them,
trailing the broad strings of a ribbon that
occasionally tripped her and rolled her to
earth.

" You poor, sad thing!" said Margaret, re-
tying the silk so jauntily around its neck
that the starved form of the cat was hardly
discoverable in the midst of her exterior
splendors. "Don't you think she's gaining
a little, Plantagenet? She was almost dead
when I took her. She would come, she
would stay, she would get in somehow."

"She's plumpin' up, you can tell by her
liveliness."

"Oh, she's dreadfully lively! She has
broken my clock already, and some other
things. I used to say I never would be an
old woman living with a cat—but you see!"

Plantagenet looked wistfully at her. With
the soft, white shawl half escaped from her
head, and the wind making havoc in her
beautiful hair, she looked so young that the
commander-in-chief laughed merrily.

" Oh, Plantagenet!"

" Did you wash to-day?"

" Yes, I washed—and made cake."

" You won't feel so old to-morrer, when you git rested."

" I don't know.  I wish you would not go on progress any more !"

" But I got to," said he, very sadly and gravely, winding a black rag with heroic firmness around an injured toe; " they all did, ye know."

" But I wish you would hold Dumbarton Castle for a while.  I am so afraid something will happen while you're gone."

" Well," said Plantagenet, glowing almost to bursting, " I will!  I'll stay and hold it a while."

Margaret's shawl drooped over him as they came towards the house.  She had a key of the back door, and they went up the stairs together, the kitten following trippingly in her again loosened ribbon.  Margaret thrust her into her own kitchen and locked the door on her, and they went on.

" We'll run to Sanctuary, won't we ?" said she.

"Yes," said Plantagenet, again swelling; "I guess we will!"

Up two flights more they climbed and knocked at a door in the attic.

"Coom ye in! Coom ye in!

"What have they been doin' to ye two?" said Granny Stuart, pluming in her chair like a hen over hawk-endangered chickens. Granny never asked of a refugee, "What have you been doing?" Never. But always, "What have they been doing to you?"

"Nothing," said Margaret, sitting down on a stool, to which she seemed very much accustomed; "we just wanted to see you."

"Has old Jusson Sprague been chasin' ye to marry him, because ye're poor and he owns the tiniments and many more?"

"No," said Margaret, obediently, from her stool on one side of Granny.

"Has O'Ragan Stuart been beatin' ye?"

"No, ma'am," replied Plantagenet from the stool on the other side.

"Then why are ye all wind-blown, my darlin'?" said Granny, patting Margaret with one hand; "and why are ye lookin' more like

a scarecrow nor iver, poor darlin'?" patting
the commander-in-chief with the other.

"Why, I just been on a little progress to-
day, Granny, and she come to meet me."

"God bless her! God bless her!" Granny's soft old hand went "pat, pat" on Margaret's head. " Ye must have a bit o' cordial,
the two o' ye."

She rose, leaning on them both, for no
one could get the cordial but she, and hob-
bled to her cupboard. Into two handleless
earthen cups she poured an equal measure
compounded with a teaspoon, and Margaret
sipped from her stool and Plantagenet sipped from his stool. It smacked of no quality libellous to temperance; no one knew
what it was but Granny, but it was the most
ecstatic mixture mortal tongue could taste.

As they sat thus in the Elysian Fields of
enjoyment, Granny between them, crooning
beautiful old-time tales, with that film over
her faded eyes that wrung both their hearts
with aching tenderness, little Pat appeared
at the door.

"Mammy wants ye, Pleg!"

They laughed him to scorn. " Yer mammy niver sint that word up here!" said Granny, sternly. And it was true. O'Ragan Stuart himself, on those rare occasions when the festive cup had obscured his senses so he could only sprawl on his hands and knees to his mother's room — to Granny — was safe even from the shadow of connubial reproach. Pat slunk away just in time to avoid his mother, bearing a tray.

And she was the embodiment of gracious smiles—unaffected smiles—true, valiant sympathy. "Has any one whativer, anywheres, been a-scoldin' of you, Plontogonet, my son?" she inquired, stoutly.

" No, mammy."

" Well for them! If a son of mine, that's descinded from such a descint as he is, can't go on a bit o' progriss like his perginnitors afore him, and take his bit ratinue along, widout a little haythen Bamboo o' a schooltacher, that niver had a candle blissed to her sowl, sindin' down here to know the why and the whyfore of it, then *I'll* be askin' the why and the whyfore too; and I'll ask it, begorry, so she'll know whose voice it is a-spakin'!"

With this she set down the tray.

"There's enough for the three o' ye; and the mate," said Mrs. O'Ragan, blushing proudly, "is drissed wid a bit o' onion. Take your enj'yment! Sure ye're like three pays in the one pod! and I big Mrs. Stuart's pardon for iver callin' her a bit o' a Bamboo. She's one of us intirely."

Thus was the universal aspect of things changed by the safe occupation of Sanctuary. Still beaming beneficently, Mrs. O'Ragan departed.

Margaret had grown used to the ornamentation of meat with an onion; she frequently clothed her own that way now, fancying, by experience, that it provided more enduring sustenance, and with her heart resolutely set to a stainless past.

The three revelled in the enjoyment to which Mrs. O'Ragan had referred them. Granny told more tales, at some of which they wept, at some of which they laughed; but in either case Margaret lifted her own dainty handkerchief to wipe the tears from Granny's cheeks—for the lifting of her arms to that height was a painful inconvenience to Granny.

"Now for the cake!" said Margaret, and ran lightly down the stairs to fetch it.

On opening the door she was met by a flood of water. The kitten — the kitten whom she had taken unwillingly, but without question or reproach, from the very scum of society and the throes of starvation—this kitten, with playful, investigating paws, had turned both faucets over the sink, which she had left spotlessly dry; her four loaves of cake were submerged, disintegrated in watery waste; the floor itself was becoming a lake.

"Isaac!" she called, with instant indifference to formalities, hearing a step in the hall below. Isaac bounded up the stairs, turned off the water, seized all the mop-rags available.

"I'll have it up before it leaks through the floor. I'll see to it!" cried this descendant of Abraham, cheerfully, his fine linen already clinging limply to his wrists.

Margaret's first thought had been that it
was an occasion of important peril.   She
rushed to Agnes.   " Oh, Agnes, my kitchen
is all in a flood; the kitten turned on the
water.   Isa — Mr. Gilchrist is mopping it.
My four loaves of cake !"

" Have dey been also washed ?"

" Oh yes."

" Dar' ! I am so glad; for I have made
you one loaf of cake dis mornin', and I t'ink
you shall have so much you will not weesh
it.   Now you shall take it."   It was already
forced into Margaret's hands.   " Now I will
go help my dear young mans."

Margaret appeared at the door, awe-struck
and awe-inspiring as the indirect author of
a considerable dilemma, holding her skirts
chastely from the indiscriminate wreckage
on the floor.   " What shall *I* do ?"

" Not'ing—you go 'way!   It shall make
you seeck."

" It is very damp.   I would not come in
here just now," said Isaac, wringing his mop
in an original but effective manner.   " It is
very malarious in here just now," he laugh-

ed; "and," he added, very kindly and seriously, "you know I am very anxious about you all the time."

Margaret blushed with her old brightness and bit her lip. "I do not know," said she, tapping with her boot on the floor. Then she burst out, impulsively, "I do not know how to thank you both! I do not know—"

"Go 'way!" said Agnes. "Go 'way dis minute! You shall be seeck."

Margaret returned to Granny's room with a better loaf of cake than she had ever made, or could ever aspire to make, in her life; and there, in Granny's lap, with her excess of ribbon trailing and bedraggled, and her wet form looking preternaturally thin, sat the kitten.

Margaret's eyes flashed, then she laughed. "Well, why not?" said she; "we all come!" She related the recent avalanche of events.

"Well, well, she knew no better," said Granny, very judicially, stroking the outcast. "The cake tastes like Agnes's cake." The kitten was feasting too. "So Isaac

Gilky ran to help you? This big soft chair
I'm settin' in he gav' me. I never knew
what comfort was afore, since I got rheu-
matiz. Run, Plontogonet, tell Isaac Gilky
when he's finished the flure to coom up
here!"

Margaret heard Plantagenet calling, naugh-
tily, from the lower flight, in a modulated
voice that did not reach his granny:

"Jerusalem! Mr. Jerusalem! Granny
wants ye when ye're through!"

Margaret met his return with eyes of hopeless reproach; he leered uneasily and hung
his head.

After a while Isaac came in, beautifully
renewed in linen.

"It is always an honor to be called to you,
mother," he said, with a low bow before the
ancient dame.

She chuckled melodiously, and held his
hand. "Why do not ye marry my lassie,
my son?" she said, nodding with tender
family pride towards Margaret. "Why do
not ye marry her and keep her out o' harm's
way?"

"I could not presume to that, mother." He stood frankly facing the old woman.

Plantagenet drew his stool, bustling angrily, over to Margaret's side, and she exchanged her look of reproach for one of unspeakable welcome. They sat very close together.

When Isaac turned, his look had no embarrassment. "Your kitchen is beautiful now," he said, his great dark eyes resting on her with their singularly humane and personally unmoved expression.

Plantagenet thrust his shock head against her shoulder, she put an arm around him; she was very pale.

"I seem," she said, "helplessly to impose on the kindness of a great many." Her voice was a little bitter and very cold.

"Ye're *my* fam'ly, down from Sen' Marie!" asserted Plantagenet, fiercely, "and *I'll* get yer 'states back for ye some time, and *I'll* get ye outer custerdy!" Certainly the two had the look of clinging to each other against the world.

"Oh, Granny, how could you?" Isaac

was gone, and she laid her head, broken-
hearted, in Granny's lap.

"Why, I've r'ason—I've r'ason to," said
Granny, caressingly and undismayed. "Do
not ye trust him? Do not ye trust him—
some way or 'nother? Now tell me that."

"She don't!" cried Plantagenet, wrathful
in tears. "Her and me's goin' to be king and
quane when I'm growed. It don't make no
dif'rence for age 'mongst sech like, it's for
p'litical r'asons."

"You dear little old crazy Irishman—my
darling boy," said Margaret, as they went
down the stairs together, "you must never
talk like that again! I do not like it, and I
won't have it—do you hear?"

"Yes'm," said Plantagenet, hopelessly, lifting the great, pure, desolate stars of his eyes
to her.

When she had thrust the kitten into the
kitchen before the disaster, she had also
thrown her slender purse on the table. Now,
alone, she took it up, musing. "Just fifty
cents, and the rent due Saturday. Oh heav-
ens! that *I—*"

But the purse felt strange. She opened it, and there, obscuring the residue of her own fortune, were five crisp ten-dollar notes.

"Plantagenet!" She called him back. "Have you been—oh, this will break my heart—have you been—*stealing* money and putting it in my purse? Now, by Sen' Marie—by Sen' Marie?"

"By Sen' Marie, I didn'!" said Plantagenet. It was enough; he never lied by that oath.

"Agnes!" She went to Agnes. "Have you — have you been putting *money* in my purse?"

"Navaire!" said Agnes, whose word was sufficient without oath.

"I could hardly be mistaken," said Margaret, recovering through her quick pride a diplomatic tone. "I have great confidence in Mr. Gilchrist; he would not, of course, Agnes, through however generous an impulse, venture to do—so insolent a thing?"

"My dear young mans, he is out!" said Agnes, dismounting Margaret from her high horse with simple social tenderness. "Lat

me tell you; dar is one poor Baptiste meen-
ester—you call it?—wid six childs, dat so
vary few go listen at him vary soon he lose
his place and break his heart, see?  So every
Wadnesday night at dose evenin' meet'n'—
you call it?—also I t'ink Sunday, my dear
young mans go gadder mans and boy and
girl a number and parsuade dem (I t'ink
also he gets dem ' jobs ') to listen at him."

Margaret looked searchingly at Agnes.
Agnes returned the look with beautiful fondness.  Margaret went back to her rooms.

CHAPTER IX

Margaret purposely loitered by a side
street on her way to the Herkimers next
morning until Isaac should take his usual
swing down the main road.

She gracefully, and, as it were, by chance,
intercepted him. " I fear you made a serious
mistake yesterday, Mr. Gilchrist. Doubtless
you laid your purse on my table to keep it
dry ; here it is. Have you mine?"

" Is this yours?" said Isaac, solemnly, taking out a large leathern book, worn and
masculine, and secured with a rubber band
an inch wide.

" You know that it is not. Probably mine
is lost; it is of little consequence. Here, at
least, is yours."

" But I cannot take your money, dear
Mrs. Stuart. I would indeed, if I needed it,
Heaven bless you! but I am not poor."

10

"I am poor," said Margaret, passionately, "but I cannot take *your* money!"

As he would not reach his hand to take it, she let it drop at his feet and turned to go.

He overtook her, the little bone of their contention in his hand. "Have I deserved this of you?" he said, pale, and his black eyes blazing. "I—a gentleman—who hold sacred the very ground you tread on!" The corpulent little purse was pressed back into her hand, his indignation towering over hers. "You have made some mistake; one often does. I am perfectly justified in warranting you that the contents of this purse are yours."

He raised his hat and stalked away, offended dignity in his gait. Margaret sucked in her underlip with the same childish sob her grandfather had died with at eighty.

"I'll go by the shore road," she said. "I'll sit down there and die. I do not care whether I ever get anywhere or not. Actors are born, not made," she mused, with curling lip, having found a comfortable rock to be cast away upon. "I will post it to him. How mad he can look! It is not the least in his heart, but the God of Abraham, Isaac, and Jacob helps him to look mad, I suppose." Having thus punished the absent and defenceless Israelite with the fine lash of her irony, she recovered her tone somewhat. " He ' holds sacred the ground I tread upon!' So he holds sacred the earth walked over by Mrs. Shaughnessy, Mrs. O'Ragan, Agnes—all; he makes no distinction. And he is 'goody-goody'—I do not like him."

Her eyes wandered desolately out to sea, the untamed lakes of Plantagenet's pet history in them. The whistle of a steam-launch blew, and, soon after the signal, groups of young people began to gather on the beach. Picnics were frequent and sacred in Yarmouth, and secular employments were not allowed to interfere with them.

So Mildred's form appeared conspicuously in gala dress—Jeff, in the group, as canty and loud as if he were one of the shop-hands.

" Well, if it is gone so far that they will go openly on a picnic together, Helen will

soon know," sighed Margaret. Insensibly
her form straightened; a sorrow that was
not for herself came over her face and gave
it a pensive dignity. Here were some children more vexedly tossed on the sea of life
than she herself was.

Mildred saw her; she hesitated, then
walked boldly over, flauntingly handsome.

"We're off on a little spree," she said,
rather condescendingly in her own pride of
spirits, seeing Margaret was so sad.

"You have not been to see me for a long
time, Mildred."           .

"I've been very busy."

"I see you are going to take Jeff," said
Margaret, with delusive simplicity. "You
are not going to have any more scruples."

"Yes, I am going to take him! And, no
—I am not going to kick against a little
good luck of my own, if I happen to have
it, any more! I find folks look out for
themselves in this world, and I don't know
as I'm bound to beat the crowd for holi-
ness."

"I think you might have worn to-day the

dress I gave you," said Margaret, looking wounded in her own sweetly audacious manner. "You have never yet worn it."

"I can't! I feel 'funny' about that dress. I'm going to put that on when I'm *good*. So I'm keeping it to be laid out in. I shall be good when I'm dead!"

"Like the Indians. I know. I often feel that way myself."

Mildred looked curiously at her. "You're getting peaked," she said, trying to sustain her manner of disinterested gayety.

"Not at all. Is that the whistle blowing for you?"

"Say," said the girl, bending over to her eagerly, "are things getting rocky with you?"

"No, you ridiculous child. There's the whistle again; go, if you are going."

"Oh, I'm going fast enough! I ain't going to break my heart for anybody. Say, I've made up my mind what I'd ought to do, and I'm going to do it. Jeff's a high-flyer—put it honest—and so am I, and we can have patience with each other—see?"

" You are not already married ?"

"No. We sha'n't deny it when we're married; we'll face the music. And Jeff is only waiting for me !" She tossed her head.

"I can readily believe that." Margaret's look was so sympathetic and so proud in the girl's beauty, Mildred stepped suddenly down from her attitude of defiance.

" *You* won't throw me off, will you, Mrs. Stuart ? You—you'd be my friend ?"

"I will be as good a friend to you as I know how, always, Mildred, and—I'll pray God every day to help me to be a better one."

Mildred did not look down into Margaret's white face again lest she should have foregone Jeff, the picnic, and all; she gathered up her resolution and rushed away, and with shouting, laughter, and the blowing of horns the launch swept out of sight.

Margaret arose from her supine mood and pursued her own way.

"Are you becoming melancholic, too?" said Mrs. Herkimer, wistfully, at the first sight of her.

"Never! My living depends, you know, on my capacity for chirking."

"And you do it always; but you needn't, you know," said the captain's lady, smiling wisely. "Judson has told us he's going to marry ye, if he can get ye—and he thinks he can get ye."

"Then *I* should be melancholic, and have to employ people to chirk me up. I think, on the whole, I'd rather be a chirker."

"Well, if ye could stand him, Mrs. Stuart, captain and me would be pleased. There's some we shouldn't like to think of as holding that position over Helen; but if *you* could make up your mind to it, we should all be pleased."

"That is good of you. Where is Stack?"

"Now I've got to break your heart."

"Stack!"

"No, he ain't dead. Captain's took him over to the island. He was gettin' so old, and he giv' all his victuals to the puppy; so cap'n took him over to old man Deans on the island. He'll take lovin' care of him.

But Stack seemed to understand it all—
you'd ought to seen his eyes!"

"I don't want to think of his eyes!" said
Margaret, flaming, and her lips trembling.

She stood over by the wall, by herself, a
moment, and Mrs. Herkimer had a vivid sus-
picion that she took out her handkerchief.

"Why, he wasn't human, Mrs. Stuart!"

Margaret made no reply.

"Well, I've got something else to break to
ye.  Judson's comin' over to dinner."

"It would not become me, I am sure," said
Margaret, without any emotion whatever, "to
object to any guest you might choose to invite to your house."

"Well, I wish ye'd make it kind of pleasant for him.  Ye're a woman that's been
used to everything that ever was.  If ye see
a book ye want, ye buy it without thinkin';
if a beggar asks ye for a dime, out it comes
by natur'; if yer gloves begin to look worn,
why it's the simple law and the prophets to
get new ones.  That's the way it should be.
I like it in ye.  But sometimes I see, perhaps
with winter and all comin', a kind of dilem-

my, perhaps, comin' to ye. Men—poor creatures!—have to be taken up and cared for by women, and—the Lord forgive me! but a man's a man when ye look for any comfort from 'em, and there ain't much to pick and choose."

Margaret, whose antecedents were as worldly as the best, naïvely admitted to herself that the practical tenor of this advice was sound. She met the elder Sprague at table with a forced, slight smile, which wandered, almost in its inception, into a look of frank pathos in another direction.

"Captain, how could you?"

"I know it; but that puppy imposed on the old fellow's—Christianity—there! I can't think o' no other name for Stack; and the little dogs all around yapped and worried him, and Stack never would turn on a little dog—never! But I tell ye, when the tide serves, to-morrow, I'll take ye all over to see him."

At this, Margaret, in spite of "company" and Mrs. Herkimer's observing scandal, calmly put away the choice bits of her meat, as usual.

"Too bad! too bad!" said Judson Sprague, attempting, with his usual salve of comment, to enter generally into the conversation.

"He'll be taken the best of care of," continued the captain, unheeding; "but I miss him: If it wasn't done, it never would be done. When I pushed the boat off, Mrs. Stuart, and left him, he didn't try to come. He understood, and he minded; but if ye'd seen—"

The captain, without shame, turned his head away and had recourse to his pocket-handkerchief. A short and distinct snivel was heard from this man of hardy experience and cold heart.

Margaret bit in her underlip with her own peculiar gasp of grief.

Mrs. Herkimer coughed sternly. "If you're both going to cry," said she, "I must be excused from table. I'm particularly depressed to-day, anyway. Of course Mr. Sprague and I can't expect to stand in the affections of you two along o' dogs."

"Pshaw, Nell!"

"Did you ever weep for *me*, Captain Herkimer?"

"Why, what is there to weep about ye for?"

"If you ever thought upon my sufferings, you wouldn't need to ask."

"I don't see as ye do suffer. Ye have everything ye want, and I take ye a sail every pleasant day when the tide serves."

A sigh, like the last, long-despairing breath of an autumn gust, escaped Mrs. Herkimer. "'Seein' they shall see and shall not understand,'" said she, solemnly, leading the way from the table before the captain's fatuous brain could frame a reply.

In the parlor the captain sank down with smiling comfort into one of the great chairs. There was a look of permanency about him which was like cordial to Margaret's secret soul.

"Captain Herkimer," said his lady, "I wish particularly to see you in the liberary."

"Oh, I forgot, Nell," said the captain, leaping, with a blush, to his feet, "what ye—what ye told me afore dinner!"

Mrs. Herkimer retreated with her prize of perspicuity in tow, and her manner suggested disgust and bodily chastisement. Sarcastic expostulation, however, was the only sound borne back upon the air.

Margaret did not condescend to blush. She faced her companion easily, with a little ripple of cool laughter.

So ostensibly left to his designs, the plutocrat of Yarmouth did not, however, waver. He had the captain's lack of astute perception, without his ingenuousness.

"I am glad that chance has offered me this gracious opportunity," he said, mellifluously.

"I ascribe it, frankly," said Margaret, a gleam of laughter still slightly disclosing her white teeth, "to Mrs. Herkimer's good generalship."

"Ah, too bad! But surely you will be serious with me when I lay my heart at your feet and ask you to marry me?"

"And would you be serious in asking me to marry you, knowing that I have no regard whatever for you?"

"Ah, most serious; for I should make it the blissful occupation of my existence to win that regard."

"I think the less time you devoted to the purpose the more likely you would be to succeed," said Margaret, in simple self-defence, induced by the horror of his ingratiating leer.

"Ah, you shall be as cruel as you like, dear Mrs. Stuart, only say 'Yes'."

"I cannot do that," said the lady, with sudden determination, "but I will consider your very kind expressions. I will think of what you have said," she added, restlessly. "Will you excuse me? I must be on my way home."

"Am I to congratulate you?" said Mrs. Herkimer, with low-voiced gravity, at the door.

"Yes, on my present escape."

The captain's lady indulged in surreptitious mirth. "I know ye wouldn't bite at the first fly. But Judson can fish as patient as the foolishest of 'em."

The captain was farther on, at the gate.

His smile was fatherly and, under the circumstances, idiotic.

"Wal, ye got it all fixed up?" he inquired,
with heroic cheerfulness.

"No, it was another exhibition of my en-
counter with the eel. I screamed and ran
away."

"I'm dum glad on it—dum!" said the hero
of the seas, revelling in untamed English in
the absence of his spouse, "for your sake!
For Helen's sake, and ourn, I wish ye could.
I don't want to spread reports about Judson
—but, slippery? Yes, sir; some of his trans-
actions have been slippery. Jeff's honest,
but he's onsteady. I don't bite that way for
Helen so fierce as Nell does." He sighed.

Margaret did not say that if she married
Judson Sprague she was likely to be mother-
in-law to Duds Sen' Tammy of the lobster
factory, rather than to the heiress of the Herkimers.

"When is the picnic launch in?" she asked.
The captain was a recognized time-table on
the incoming of all craft.

"Due at seven; but when them high-flown

birds o' plumage from the shops get off, I always allow 'em an extra hour for flutin' and sand-gallopin'."

Drawn by some irresistible impulse, Margaret found herself, by moonlight, on the rock where she had been cast away in the morning, still waiting for the boat-signal. It came, alarmingly tardy, and jubilantly defiant of the fact. Margaret thought the gayety of some vinously irresponsible, and their steps marked by a suspicious irresolution.

Among this latter number Mildred and Jeff emerged and came digressively, without yet seeing her, towards the cluster of rocks where she sat.

Jeff carried a market-basket in which jelly-tumblers, or champagne-bottles, or both, clattered noisily as he walked, without his particular observation. Mildred lurched against him, to her own self-astonishment, and they both laughed with endearing good-nature.

"Hide basket here in rocks till nex' picnic," said Jeff. "Beg pardon! Oh, Mrs.

Stuart! How d' ye do? 'Lighted!" Jeff
gave his cap a low sweep.

Mildred looked as though she had seen a
ghost. "Been here, deares' friend, all day?"
she inquired, with great *aplomb*, however.

"Shall be 'lighted t' see two such lovely
ladies home," said Jeff, the color in his genial,
boyish face not disparaged by the coldness
of the moonlight.

"Jeff," said Mildred, severely, her beautiful hair tossed about her Madonna-like features, "I won't have it! We'd make holy
show o' 'rselves. You take Mrs. Stuart. I
go home 'lone!"

"Goin' to see you home. Don't care a
damn!" said Jeff; a true Lochinvar, in spite
of difficulties.

"Go as quietly straight home as you
can," said Margaret, who had risen, laying
her hand in sane admonishment on Jeffrey's
shoulder. "I will see Mildred home."

CHAPTER X

MARGARET felt that she had reason to doubt whether the willingness of Mildred and Jeff to excuse each other's delinquencies would much conspire, on the whole, to their mutual benefit.

Mildred was in such a state that she had brought her to her own room, covering, with the alert secrecy of a sister, her unsteady progress up the backstairs.

"Good-night, deares' friend," Mildred had said with the utmost complacency, accepting at once the proffered comforts of Margaret's bed. So Margaret had propped herself in her chair by the fire. The girlish face on the pillow, as she glanced at it now and then, was so chaste in feature and so free from any mark of dissipation, she found it hard to believe that Mildred had gone, that night, to the extent of actual intoxication.

11

At all events, her heart was as savagely maternal over her as over her other wandering star, Plantagenet. No one should know, no one should accuse, no one should reproach.

Present defence rather than mental analysis of the misdoings of her friends, was Margaret's attitude; wherein she and Granny Stuart, in her "Sanctuary" up-stairs, did indeed seem members corporate of one immemorial family.

"What have they been doin' to ye, my quane, darlin'?" For Margaret, restless herself, seeing Mildred safely sleeping, and knowing that Granny's lamp was burning, had softly made her way thither over the tenement stairs in a dressing-gown fit for a princess. Margaret was getting reduced to some of her finest apparel.

"What have they been doin' to ye?"

"Oh, Granny, I love to come to you even when I'm not abused!"

If she had been born of Granny's own self, a fiercer love-light could not have flamed in the faded old eyes. "Well ye

may! The first day ye came, Bridget O'Ragan cam' up here to me. 'She's a bamboo,'
says she. 'Whish!' says I, 'I see her come
up the path. She's a Stuart,' says I. 'What's
her name?' says I. 'Stuart,' says she." Granny chuckled with spring-time laughter.

"'Her husband's did,' says she, 'wid no
insurance on him. Her two babbies wint
afther, like aingil sirruphs, callin' Daddy,'
says she. 'She had a millen dollars in the
banks,' says she, 'and thim as counts it over
ivery Satherday night grapped it up—the
thaves! and rinned away wid it. No hide
or hair to thim was iver found,' says she."

Margaret listened in stupefied admiration
throughout to this unconscious testimony to
Mrs. O'Ragan's glories in the line of fictional
art.

"But it was not that way at all, Granny,
dear."

"Niver mind! niver mind!" said Granny,
still on fire, and unheeding. "I'll see ye
blissed yet, I will!"

The old face became at once softened and
broodingly wise. For Granny was no com-

mon old woman ; she had tremendous ideals ; she had a heart unzoned by any earthly circumference.

Isaac Gilchrist heard three raps of Granny's poker on her wood - box. Margaret thought she was merely tightening the handle of that article. Margaret knew some of the signals of the tenements, but not all. She was not even alarmed by the fact that Granny took off her apron with the plain button in the back and put on the white one with strings. Isaac had received by the post that night a package, whose authorship he instantly divined; he knew the contents before he opened it, and he seemed to dread to open it.

At last he did so, possessed by the vision of a note, perhaps, wafting the same elusive perfume, some gracious words commensurate with his own ardor of simple loyalty.

But there was no note; there was only the sordid fact of the fifty dollars.

Slowly he unbound the leathern book and put the notes therein. With extreme patience he folded the wrapper with the hand-

writing, and that he placed deliberately,
with persevering care, in the breast-pocket
of his coat.

He then took an attitude before his fire,
with both hands clasped about his knees,
and, without paper or pen, pursued for a
long time his desolate researches into human philosophy.

It was thus that he heard Granny rap
three times with her poker on her wood-
box.

"Poor old mother!" said he, rising. "She's
in trouble for somebody. It's never herself
—grand old soul!"

So he sprang up the stairs and rapped at
the door.

"Coom ye in! Why — it's Isik!" said
Granny, with a diplomatic surprise worthy
of worldlier circles.

Isaac smiled; he never betrayed a lady.
Margaret looked pathetically glorious on
her stool in Granny's poor little room.

"I came to say good-night, mother. You
must pardon my coming so late—I was very
busy."

"I'll pardon yer comin' late, but niver yer goin' without a word, Isik."

So Isaac took Plantagenet's stool. The news of the day, the weather, his constant interest in both ladies—on all these themes he discoursed in his usual calm manner.

Margaret, in Granny's immediate proximity and leaning against her chair, had at first regarded him with eyes in which a hint of contemptuous triumph was not easily concealed.

As he continued to meet her look so gravely and unconsciously, with unintermitted kindness, she grew safely piqued.

"Did you receive it back?" said the great eyes from the queenly head leaning against Granny's chair. "Do you not think I have won? I usually win. Are you not punished for your insolence?"

But the Jew pursued the even tenor of his way.

"One o' ye comes to me, and then the ither comes to me!" said Granny, gladly, unobservant of all tactics save her own. "Some time ye'll be comin' to me togither!"

Margaret laughed slightly, without regard, as though she were at some small theatre condoning the crudeness of the actors.

" Here, take her, my son !" continued Granny, aloud, in the uninterrupted flow of her innocent aspirations—" take her to the priest and marry her. *She's* fit for ye! Come and take her, I say, and take keer o' her. She's wurstlin' wi' the world, poor darlin', and she's no fit to wurstle wi' the world."

" Granny — Granny, you are going too far!" Margaret drew her head back, colorless.

" Not to - night, mother," said Isaac, very calmly, rising. " Yes, I will take her to the priest and marry her, but not to-night."

He held out his hand to Granny and bowed low over hers. He held out his hand, firm, unshrinking, warm, to Margaret. She turned from him and went to the window. So he bowed where she had stood, and without one glance of understanding with Granny thereafter—so grave a gentleman was he —left the room.

Margaret, standing frigid by the window,

heard a sob. She turned. Yes, there was the film over Granny's old eyes.

"I wouldn't hurt a hair o' yer sweet head! I loove ye! I loove ye!"

That straining film, the heart-broken catching of the breath in one so old, so infinitely loving—though Granny had humbled her to the dust, Margaret would have rushed to her, stung by such compunction, put her arms about her and taken to her own cheeks the tears from those withered ones.

"Ye should no' be so highty-tighty, little one! I been a lang, lang journey in this auld world. I worked a lang, lang stent in it afore me auld honds failed me. I seen mony men and mony things. There's no mony men like Isik. When I was a little girl like you, I seen the rivers rollin' in a far, far land—"

Granny's old mind was moving, as it did sometimes, in large rather than distinct areas.

"A little girl like me! Oh, look at me, Granny!" Margaret laughed tenderly through her own tears.

"Aye, so ye be! But I don't worry of ye any more. Isik 'll keep hairm from ye. He b'langs to Holy Church. He don't know it, the chiel, but he b'langs. So do ye, but ye're no' so true to the faith as Isik, my poor darlin'. No, ye're no' so true to yer faith as Isik."

"There is one promise, at least," thought Margaret, going down the stairs, "that 'Isaac' will never be held accountable for!"

Granny's model young man heard the soft swish of that descending dress. His black eyes glowed exultantly, as though his hearth-fires were already kindled.

Margaret, after another shielding look at the erring beauty on her bed, composed herself again in her chair as best she could.

## CHAPTER XI

MARGARET slipped out early to her kitchen to prepare a breakfast. She left the door ajar lest Mildred should escape unobserved —a thing which that young woman, with a face of dark despair, came very near doing.

"Mildred, come! Help me! I'm in such a mess!"

Margaret's house-keeping was always conveniently — and that without much affectation—serving the purposes of tragedy.

"The bacon fat's on fire!"

Mildred subdued this holocaust, but there was a fire of shame on her own face not so easily vanquished.

"I little thought," said Margaret, "that, because I happened to have a very plain breakfast, you would not sit down and eat it with me." And the reproach in her eyes was for this present inhumanity of treatment, and for nothing else.

"I've had your bed all night, now you want me to eat your breakfast."

"Once," said Margaret, "there was a certain woman went down by boat to Yarmouth, and thereupon she fell deadly ill, and a certain dear girl with a great big heart gave her her own nest in the cabin, and made her warm, and cured her headache, and sat up herself all night long."

The tears began to run down Mildred's cheeks and fall on her burnt bacon, which was already exceedingly bitter.

"You'll pity me and be good to me, but you won't love me any more."

Margaret rushed over from her chair and practically demonstrated the falsehood of this statement by a warm and tenacious embrace.

"I never did—that thing before," sobbed the girl. "Jeff didn't take it out of the cellar, though—he bought it himself!"

"Well, that is something to be proud of, at least."

"And we were th-thirsty, and it did t-taste nice; but it's like everything else—you have to c-cry in the end."

"I know it," said Margaret, with a look only of the clearest sympathy. "I wish I were unselfish and good, so I could talk to you about self-denial and spurning temptation. But I will only tell you that when I discovered you down at the beach last night, and when you lay there on the bed, it just about broke my heart; for I've always been so proud of you, and ever since the first time I saw you, you know, it has seemed as though you belonged to me."

"*I* seemed to belong to you?"

"Why, certainly. Nothing in the world could ever alter that."

"I guess," said Mildred, rising with a sudden intimation of buoyancy where she had been downcast and confused, "if I ever touch that stuff again, it 'll be poisoned first and set on fire! But see here! could—could things be getting a little rocky, perhaps, for you to stand?"

"Nonsense! Do you think you *deserved*

a sumptuous breakfast this morning? Run along to your work, and do not criticise the means I have seen fit to use for your chastening."

Never had Margaret's laugh sounded merrier. When Mildred was gone, however, she leaned her head on the table in dreary apprehension:

"'Rocky'? Oh, what is this coming to? Yesterday I found it pecuniarily convenient to purchase only three rolls, and the shopgirl had the good-natured, unconscious heartlessness to ask me if I 'was not taking big chances?' What is it all—"

"For'erd, march! Folly yer leader!" called the voice of the captain of the "Pluck and Liver Corps"; and with an ever-ready aspiration to be diverted somehow from her sorrows, Margaret rose and went to the window.

She was astonished to be the only visible spectator of the painfully elaborated scene there in progress. The mature occupants of the tenements being mostly employed in the rear at this hour, Plantagenet was fearlessly re-enacting some of the bloodiest of

barbaric annals in the very front of Catholic
Christendom.

The dirty and wondering little Kate
Shaughnessy—six years comprised her earthly experience — was erected upon a scaffold,
which consisted exclusively of an inverted
wash-tub, time-worn and inclined to sprawl,
and poised on the rim of this same tragic
elevation stood Tommy Sullivan, brandish-
ing the executioner's axe, a weapon composed
in this case, as Margaret rejoiced to see, simply of a broad chip, tied, with the natural
indecision of a white cotton string, to a
broom handle.

But even this was not intended to descend
upon Katie.  She represented Sen' Marie
Stuart, whom Plantagenet, taking the se-
quel of his chosen history deliberately into
his own hands, was about to rescue.

The marvelling Katie had, in a less interesting hour of the morning, stolen a cucumber from a neighboring garden; it was too
large for the pocket of the one garment she
wore, and she now grasped its exposed portion
convulsively with her broad red little hand,

as a safeguard against the astounding events
of time.

"For'erd, march! Folly yer leader!" It
was not as a pedestrian that Plantagenet appeared at this proud crisis. As the troop, to
the clatter of several tin-pail covers and
one diseased mouth-organ, swung round the
corner of the house to the rescue, Margaret
beheld her boy, the remnants of "H. M. S.
*Mohawk*" courageously flaunting one ear,
seated on his own mother's cow.

The cow, accustomed to being led, followed
in demure obedience the one small and wicked
boy at the other end of her halter, whose
trousers were held in place by a meat skewer.
As the cavalcade approached, Katie's immu-
table wonder changed instantly to a thoroughly sensible yell of distinct distress. The boy
with the skewer halted the cow at the block,
where she bent at once to an unperturbed
search for grass. Plantagenet reached over
to draw up Marie Stuart, alias Katie, to his
saddleless mount. She resisted lustily. In
view of execution she had maintained a
calm, even an awesomely expectant atti-

tude, but she naturally objected to being
rescued.

In the frantic struggle, the top of the
wash-tub caved in, and Katie went with it;
the cow, startled at last both by the spectacle and the crash, lifted her head, swung
her tail, and flung out to the highway with
Plantagenet clinging dauntlessly to her neck.
The army, without the slightest regard for a
long-sustained course of martial discipline,
tore after Plantagenet and the cow. And
ere Margaret could descend to a wholly in-
formal rescue of the *quasi* queen, both Mrs.
O'Ragan and Mrs. Shaughnessy stood on the
spot.

"'Tis a fine lot o' milk yer coo 'll be giv-
in' the night, Bridget, wid that divil of a
Pleg ridin' the poor domesthic cr'atur' all
over town on his haythen progrissions!"

Mrs. O'Ragan had this thought herself
and was wrathy; but at this sally, the point
of her anger turned.

"Sure I can't hilp it at all, if my childern
is that will descinded they be rampajus wid
the glory of it. It's not her coo a thruc

mother's heart 'u'd be thinkin' of, it's her darlin' child."

"Oh," cried Mrs. Shaughnessy, with a sarcastic laugh, "I lay yer worry, then. Never fear. Pleg Stuart 'll get home safe to his supper though he's drowndit by sea, and flailed by land. 'Tis poor little innercents like my Katie is in danger o' bein' kilt by the likes o' him. Will ye have a bit o' salt on yer fruit, my sweet lamb?" said Mrs. Shaughnessy, straining Katie to her bosom, who, in turn, had renewed her embrace of her cucumber.

"If ye allow yer child to ate a grane melon o' that size — espicially one that she's broke God's holy law by st'alin', don't be layin' the dith of her to my Pleg!" said Mrs. O'Ragan.

Mrs. Shaughnessy set Katie down and squared off. Mrs. O'Ragan was drawing her waist-cable to the seeming point of belligerency, when a dapper form appeared in the distance which drew the absorbing gaze of both.

"'Tis old Sprague for his rint. The low-

12

ness of him! to go around collectin' of his own rints!"

"Thrue for ye, Bridget Stuart. 'Tis a thrue word ye're sp'akin'."

"I hope yer headache is betther to-day, Kate Shaughnessy."

"Much better, Mrs. O'Ragan Stuart, ma'am—thank ye, kindly."

"Come in and have a sup o' tay wid me, Mrs. Shaughnessy, ma'am. I was jist puttin' the same to draw on the stove whin Plontogonet distressed me so wid his behavior. Faith, he's a - wearin' the life o' me."

"Plontogonet's a fine, handsome boy as iver stipped abroad, and 'll soon be out-growin' his bit o' wildness."

In sweet amicability, the two climbed the steps together, Katie following with her cucumber, her round face wearing its normal expression of blank astonishment.

Margaret, whose rooms were sublet to her by Mrs. O'Ragan, had no dealing with the rent-collector, and not desiring to meet him on the way out, she waited till he should

STUART AND BAMBOO                    179

have made his departure before starting on
her walk to the Herkimers.

But he anticipated her by an emissary—
no less than Mrs. O'Ragan herself, in a state
of disgust.

"'Tis old Sprague has been skinnin' us of
our rint again, Mrs. Stuart, dear; and he
says he has a missage for you from Mrs.
Herkimer, so I sint him in me parlor, knowin' I could sphrinkle it wid holy wather after
I have it rid of the prisence of him."

"Won't you sprinkle a little over me before I go down?" said Margaret, meeting the
other's eyes with full solemnity.

"Oh, darlin' one, when ye come back to
the church that loves ye, ye shall have an
annointin'—niver forget!"

Margaret opened the "parlor" door and
stood leaning against it. Her attitude ex-
pressed not so much dislike as a weary indifference.

"Mrs. Herkimer wished me to remind you
that she is expecting you. Oh, why should
you be at anybody's call, you beautiful creature!" Judson broke off, but in a scrupu-

lously soft voice. "Too bad! too bad!
Why should you suffer when there are pro-
tecting arms open to receive you?"

He spread his cuffs abroad and even approached her. Her eyes, twice their natural
size, were as full of pure horror and specula-
tion as Plantagenet's when he saw uncanny
aspects at night after a misspent day.

Judson was not flattered by this regard,
but he thought it a good time to proceed.

"Why will you not drop the burden and
let me bear it for you? Ah, you must! I
have the intimation—the intimation of love
—that you cannot bear the burden much
longer. Let it fall. Let it fall, sweet one,
and be buried in my heart."

Margaret, still with her wide, spectre-see-
ing eyes, caught her breath in her own peculiar sob.

"There, there! I ask you to make no
demonstration — not even a word. I will
simply call you mine—and I forever your
slave. Why should you be so proud? And
yet I wish you proud. Not a word! not a
word! You look very pale and—tired. Let

the day for our marriage be as early as possible. Farewell, my own, farewell!"

"'Pale and *hungry*,' he was going to say," thought Margaret, and reaching her room, laughed, and then lay back in her chair trembling.

"I am *not* engaged to him. He is like an ugly spell; he enthralled my imagination in a moment of weakness and faintness. Oh, Isaac! Isaac! Isaac! I trust *you!* I almost I— But to be taken up as an incompetent by you, to be cared for out of pity—never! never! I will marry Judson Sprague first, and show you that there can be glaciers as cold as yourself."

## CHAPTER XII

"Blisséd Saint Anthony" — Margaret heard Mrs. O'Ragan in the hall—"I've lost me coo!"

It was only one phase of the flexible strain, "Blessed Saint Anthony, I've lost me glasses!" or "Blessed Saint Anthony, restore me me choppin'-tray!" or whatever.

Never was a patron saint more indulgent; and, as she was going out, Margaret was not surprised to hear, "Thanks to blisséd Saint Anthony, Mrs. Stuart, dear, me coo's restored."

' "And Plantagenet?"

"The b'ys say, when the coo shook him off he borryd a dory along shore and put off on a progriss to the island—the gall o' him!"

"People ought not to lend a dory to such a young boy alone."

"Blame no one, dear, for none was nigh.

He borryd it free and aisy, like thim kings
and quanes afore him, begorry; and coy he'll
be about comin' in and lavin' it on the beach,
and then rin to his granny. 'Tis a regular
thayeter I'm livin' in, and not like the mither
of a baptized family at all. God help me!"

"Blessed Saint Anthony! blessed Saint
Anthony!" murmured Margaret, on her way
to the Herkimers, "do not let me lose my
heart! One can bear all things if one does
not lose one's heart. A Christian has no af-
finity for a Jew, though sometimes—now—"
she bit her lip as warmly as though there
had been any one near to see her confusion—
"it does comfort me that he is always 'so
anxious about me'—'so anxious about me'!"

As for Plantagenet, she felt a bit of family
pride in the dauntless way he was conserving
the talents of the primitive aristocracy—since
Mrs. Shaughnessy had said, "By sea or land
he would come home safe to his supper"; for
Margaret had another wayward impulse—to
feel that the light would go out of her life if
she should lose Plantagenet.

When, at evening, the "tide served," she

preceded the Herkimers—with whom she was
to take the promised sail to the island to see
Stack—in a stroll to the beach.

But there was no sail to the island that
night. Stack was coming home. He had
stayed loyally and uncomplainingly; but now
he had a good excuse, and he was coming
home. In the distance Margaret saw him,
and he was holding a tawny head that she
knew above the waves.

Plantagenet's "borrowed" craft, ill-ma-
nœuvred in the mounting sea, had upset him
as he pursued his homeward trip. Stack,
looking wistfully across, had seen the boy
clinging to the boat and drifting outward,
and had himself, with the last swift exertion
of his old age, organized a rescue. He was
coming home with the hero of many adventures, himself to be a sublimated hero at last.

Margaret looked wildly about her. She
saw Helen coming down the lane in advance
of her father and mother, and ran to her.
"Plantagenet is drowned!" she said, her face
perfectly colorless, "and Stack is bringing
him home! Run—run for Isaac!"

" Isaac ?"

" Isaac Gilchrist! He can save him, if there is any hope! Oh, Helen, run!"

" Where ?"

" In the place where I live! Take the short cut over the cliffs! He may be nearer!—he may be on the road! He is usually coming home at this hour! Oh, run! run!"

" Go meet my father! He can save them in the boat if Stack gives out!" cried Helen, reasonably, and then ran as she was bid.

" Plantagenet is dead!" gasped Margaret, meeting the captain. " Stack is bringing him home—the boat!"

But before the captain had reached the beach and could board his dory, Stack, bravely, desperately swimming, was too near for that aid ; so he did it all himself. He brought Plantagenet in, and he himself lay panting on the beach.

" Yes, the boy's gone, I'm afraid," said the captain, dolefully shaking his head ; " but I might try."

But Margaret had taken the drowned body in her arms, sheltering it almost fiercely. She

had seen the lids close over too many be-
loved eyes. In extremities she had never,
now, any hope of life; so she held the limp
form when Isaac came bounding to them
over the cliffs.

"Give him to me!" he said. Margaret
shook her head, the tears running piteously
down her cheeks and dropping on Plantagenet's streaming curls.

With gentlest force Isaac loosened the boy
from her grasp, and, with swift action, and
orders to those not too despairing to assist
him, in no long time he had the briny deep
pumped out of Plantagenet and the breath
of life faintly heaving in him again.

"Sure as I'm a sinner the little devil's
breathin'!" cried the captain, in unbelieving
joy, while Margaret's face went from pallor
to an amazing rose color.

"Let us remember, captain," his lady ad-
jured him, "that we've just been standin' on
the brink of eternity."

"I supposed the boy'd pitched over," responded the captain, cheerfully. "If it
hadn't been for that—Jew?"—he indicated

the place where Isaac was still leaning over Plantagenet.

"Yes," said Margaret, and very proudly. Jew or Christian, it was sufficient to her mind to have a knight who could bring the dead to life.

No one had much noticed the old dog, Stack, nor had he thought of his own condition, gazing with all his heart at the efforts to restore this last trophy of his magnanimity and prowess. But now it was evident that it was Stack, and not Plantagenet, who was dying.

When the captain saw this he went and stood over him with a pale face, and his lady took her place in unreproachful sympathy at his side. But Stack's solemn eyes were turned full upon Margaret, and with a sharp pang of remorse and love she went over and encircled his wet, shaggy neck with her arms.

Then came the last conversation they ever had together, and it was a brief one—an inaudible but clearly understood language of the eyes.

"I am very sorry for you," said Stack,

utterly unselfish to the last; "it is hard for
you to see me die."

At this Margaret gave him a look which
opened without further pain the ascending
gates of life to him.  For, as she pressed her
sweet face against his, already cold, the struggle was over.

"I wish you to come with me, if you will"
—she heard Isaac's kind voice.  "I am going to take the boy home.  Come!"

She rose vaguely but obediently.  With
Plantagenet in his arms, and Margaret at his
side, it was a strangely assorted, remarkable-
looking company that started up the cliff
path home.

Now that the stray lamb's arms hung so
limp over Isaac's shoulder, Margaret saw
how the boy had grown of late, and that his
jacket and trousers, though never so gener-
ously supplemented with fortunate bits of
fabric, impartial in color and design, had
still been unable to keep pace with the swift
evolutions of time.

Moreover, Isaac, though so strong, was of
slender build, and the resistless members of

this lost one of the flock seemed to surround him, crayfish-like. And in this manner he whom Plantagenet had so often and wilfully called "Jerusalem," bore the Catholic prince of the house of Stuart very carefully and tenderly up the steeps.

The rescued one himself, though so weak, was proud — nothing less. To have been overturned in a dory betwixt shores, to have been in deathly peril, and to have been towed ashore by a dog—it was a consummation of bliss that sat nobly on his features.

"Granny!" he demanded, faintly, and Margaret and Isaac nodded.

This was the evening hour when the free-born of the tenements rallied one another from their front door-steps. The trio crept softly up the dark backstairs.

"What have they been doin' to ye, my lamb?" cried Granny.

"A wicked boat overturned him," said Isaac, without perceptible sarcasm; "a noble dog saved him."

"God rest his sowl!" said Granny, fervently, irrespective of race or kind, and raised her eyes and crossed herself.

"Have you just a bit of beef, Agnes?" said Margaret, appearing at that matron's door. "I happen to be out, and I need it at once for some one who is ill."

It was given eagerly.

"And will you come and help me make it into beef-tea, Agnes?"

"We shall mek it right here upon my keetchen fire. Yours, maybe, iss gone out."

It was out, indeed, and Margaret was well content not to have the poverty of her larder revealed. In the general excitement Mrs. Herkimer had not paid her for the few hours of chirking she had been able to render that day. She had given her last dollar for rent, and her home meals were consisting exclusively of toast from accumulated fragments of bread. But she went up the stairs happy with her steaming bowl of tea.

"Oh, you are a genius!" said Isaac.

He knew the moment he looked at it that it was a concoction of Agnes's own, and Margaret was conscious that he knew, but his

commendation was so vivid and tender she
accepted it with a simply reflected triumph
in her tired, wide eyes.

Isaac had Plantagenet bathed and in clean,
dry clothes, lying on his granny's lounge, sip-
ping "cordial."

Margaret had never seen her young rela-
tive clean and thoroughly brushed before.
His recent experiences had made his high-
born features eminently pale, and she stood
gazing at him—herself thin and toast-fed—
in pleased surprise.

"There! Isik, be they mother and child,
or be they not?"

Isaac smiled. "They are both of your own
superb family, mother."

"And have you taken her to the priest yet,
Isik?"

"Not yet, mother."

"But ye will?"

"Oh, surely; all in good time, mother."

Margaret was giving Plantagenet his tea,
with her back happily turned to this dialogue. The boy saw her face go from red
to white and white to red.

" Jerusalem's a brick," he whispered, tears in the desolate beauty of his eyes. " I'm too young. You—you can have him."

" Thank you, dear," said Margaret, coldly, all her dignity returning to her.

When she went out Isaac followed her.

" Now he will propose to me," she thought, " in order to feed me! And I must refuse him." But her heart beat violently.

Isaac, however, reflected none of her agitation as he walked methodically down the stairs at her side.

" What an engaging, *haunting* face that little reprobate up there has," he said.

" He is charming, now that he is bathed," said Margaret, gladly.

" We must try to do something for him," continued Isaac. " He is wonderfully bright for his station, and he certainly has the lion-heart of the race he counts his descent from. He has more life than he knows what to do with, and he is devoted to you. You could shape his energies. We must give him a chance."

Margaret's heart stood still. "We!. We! We!" swam in her brain.

But Isaac took her hand in parting, with unbroken calm. "I shall be glad when there is not so much to try you," he said. "I think of you constantly. Remember that I am always thinking of you, and always near."

"It is adorable of him not to compel me to refuse him to-night," said Margaret, in her own room. "I think it would almost have broken my heart to have to refuse him to-night."

She had deliberately put pen, paper, and ink before her, and the object of her long-suspended epistolary efforts was to write Judson Sprague.

"If Stack—if a *dog*—can give his life laboriously and painfully in a good cause, I think I can starve on toast by cheerful degrees rather than *sell* myself, simply to be supported in ease by a man I can hardly bear in my sight."

So she wrote:

"DEAR MR. SPRAGUE,—I am confident that you have deceived yourself in some inferences which you seemed

13

to draw regarding my sentiments towards you ; and I am to blame that, in a moment of mental anxiety and bewilderment, I did not tell you frankly the real conviction of my heart, that I do not care for you and that I can never marry you.

      "Very gratefully and sincerely,

                "MARGARET STUART."

## CHAPTER XIII

But Judson Sprague had determined to marry Margaret Stuart, and he chose to construe what he had imputed as a hopeful sign of concession on her part into full authority to execute his plans. A little bird in the air had told him that she entertained a friendly acquaintance with the Jew, and he resolved to nip any possible fancy of that sort discreetly and promptly in the bud.

Isaac had a bit of an office in the city, where he sat when it pleased him; and the magnates of the town, in judicious awe of the golden calf, though a closeted and unassuming one, knew that office well.

So Isaac was not surprised when Judson Sprague entered, smiling and gracious.

"Ah, you could buy us all out, Mr. Gilchrist, and you sit here as demurely as

though you and we did not know it! Ah,
too bad of you! too bad!"

"I have no desire to buy you out, Mr.
Sprague." Isaac practised carelessly with a
pencil on a scrap of paper at his side.

"No, there is nothing of the usual —
nothing of the pawnbroker about you —
nothing of the pawnbroker. We all know
that."

The Jew's dark eyes regarded the other
too gravely for reproach.

"Now I," continued Judson Sprague, and
that gayly, "though an older man—I have
more of the fever, the joy, the *animus* of
existence. Take warning, Mr. Gilchrist, and
keep in the safe seclusion of the unemotional. It is a better investment in a pecuniary
sense—ha! ha!—a better investment. Still,
I am content—I am content."

A shade of impatience passed over Isaac's
face, still absently drawing with his pencil.

"But I came here on business, Mr. Gilchrist. In order, however, that I may do
justice to my errand, and that you may understand *why* I wish to sell certain valuable

properties, I will explain, if you will allow me."

" Yes."

"I take, perhaps, a boyish pleasure in doing so. I am supremely happy. I am going to marry a most charming woman. I think perhaps you have heard of her—Mrs. Stuart—ah, Mrs. Margaret Stuart, ah!"

" Yes."

Judson Sprague wondered if the Jew was engaged in pencilling some new Levitical law, so absolutely calm was his face.

" I propose, for her sake—she is not strong —to break up my humdrum existence here for a while, to spend a couple of years in travel and residence abroad."

" Well?"

"My tenement property, Mr. Gilchrist, particularly my houses on Cliff Street, I have always found very remunerative. But that is when the owner is by to regulate, as far as possible, the contingent expenses, to modify and supervise all demands made upon him, and to look strictly after his own rents. Ah, you understand."

" Well?"

" I desire, therefore, under the flattering circumstances before alluded to, to sell this property—to get it off my hands, good gold though it is. Conditions change values. Remember, I do not regret the conditions—ha! ha!"

Isaac's face looked drawn. He made no reply.

" I come to you because, while some of us are reputed to be wealthy men, and are indeed, I trust, wealthy men, you—ah, too bad of you! but it is your way—have come, nevertheless, to control the literal finance of our banks, as it were —ha! ha! if I may so speak. And yet you live the life of a hermit. We have asked you in vain to dine with us. Ah, well, in a pecuniary sense, doubtless, it is wisdom—it is wisdom."

Isaac had taken a fresh piece of paper, upon which he drew some slight plans.

" Those are the houses you wish to sell?"

" Quite right—quite right."

Isaac, taking back the paper, made some

computations, and handed it again to Judson Sprague.

"I will give you so much. I have placed the amount there—individually and collectively."

"Ah, but, Mr. Gilchrist, you are jesting— you are jesting! Really you are taking advantage of my present disposition to sell."

"It is quite optional with you whether you will take it or not. It is my offer in price. I shall make no other."

"Ah, ah!" The sum was a little more than Judson had determined to take at the lowest. A glance at Isaac's face quieted a little his voluble tongue, and convinced him besides that, if he let this opportunity slip, he would have no other.

"Well—well—very well. So be it. Shall we step in next door and have the papers drawn?"

When Isaac returned to his office, he locked the door, drew the shades down over the windows, and shut out all the light from his eyes with his long, thin hands.

"If that be so," he said, at last, "she needs

a friend more than ever. If I could have
had time to win her trust and love! God
of my fathers! God of my fathers!"—his
heart clung desperately and with unrea-
soning simplicity, in this hour, to the power
of a mighty tradition—"God of my fathers,
turn her heart to me! I will be true to
her!"

## CHAPTER XIV

AND instead of an acceptance of her refusal came a magniloquent box of flowers from Margaret's unblushing suitor. She ate her crusts amid the odor of the choicest exotics.

And the Jew was sad when by chance she met him. "He is in love with some one," thought Margaret, "and he is sorry for me." And so she swept by distantly, her head neither more nor less proudly carried than ever.

"It is evident she has made up her mind to marry him," thought Isaac. "Perhaps she cares for him! I am a Jew—he is a Christian." He laughed, sombrely, and grew into the habit of pacing the beach a great deal with his hat pulled low over his eyes.

Plantagenet, mainly occupied in wearing out the new clothes Isaac had given him, sometimes watched him wistfully. "They're all alike, all them Sen' Marie Stuarts," he pondered. "It takes a whole rigimunt, cavulry and harkerbusses, swingin' around the cornder, to fetch 'em. *I* could git her, if I was old enough. He don't know how—he talked gamey up in Granny's room, but suthin's knocked him over. Psh! He wants to read up a little."

Isaac saw the royal, but, on the whole, compassionate, disdain on Plantagenet's features.

"Would you like to go away to school, Plantagenet? To a real military school, and wear a handsome uniform, and study like a brave boy—would you?"

"No, sir, I wouldn't. I've got some pretty funny beats around here, and I've got my own ' Pluck and Liver Kore.' "

"But would you go if Mrs. Stuart asked you?"

"Not if she asked me; but if she cried, I'd have to!"

"Does she ever cry, Plantagenet?"

"Yes, sir, she does cry."

"Oh, I thought she was one of the kind that never cried!" Isaac tried to be scoffing.

"See here!" said Plantagenet; "onct, nex' to me, you had the most sand o' anybody in Yarmouth, you had!"

"Well?"

"If you want to ketch a Stuart, you don't want to filter out on sand!"

Isaac's gloomy smile encouraged his Catholic tutor.

"Ah, but if she is going to marry somebody else, Plantagenet?"

"Who?"

"Mr. Judson Sprague, for instance."

"That roun'-toed, snifflin' ol' jelly-tumbler! No, sir."

"But he is rich, you know."

"No, sir; she won't do it."

"Why, Plantagenet?"

"I won't let her!"

"You must feel very smart, indeed, to say that."

"I be smart. I'm smart as the hull city o' Yarmouth!" Plantagenet put his new and larger "H.M.S. *Mohawk*" over one ear

and spat out a little licorice as a shining
substitute for the dignity of tobacco. "Set
yer mind easy. I won't let her—not if I
come into church with my kore and bust the
perceedin's—no, sir!"

"And would you let her marry me?"

Plantagenet wilted, his cap sought a natural level, his eyes became the solemn deso-
lations of a country loved and lost.

"Yep," he said; but with the words he
turned abruptly and took to his heels.

Margaret closed her inner door upon the
flowers—they were wearily sweet. She had
felt an increasing weakness for days—and
crusts are not sustaining. Languidly she let
the intention of walking to the Herkimers,
of bringing in her clothes from the line—
all other actual intentions—slip from her
mind.

"He would then be free from his self-im-
posed notion of loyalty, to marry whom he
liked. If I marry Judson Sprague, it will
solve all difficulties. It may be too late already to get sufficiently nourished. I do not
feel that I shall ever be hungry again."

She laughed with a fine scorn, but fever-
ishly, drew the low chair she was sitting in
to the bed, and laid her head down there.

And that, for some long weeks, was the
last of Margaret's perplexed and weary
scheming.

Towards nightfall of that day Helen came
as a deputation of inquiry from her mother,
as well as from a strong personal intuition of
trouble, and she found Margaret in the de-
lirium of a fever.

"My trunks are all packed," said the lady.
"I sail for England to-night—the climate is
so moist and cool—*cool*—and the hedges—
the hedges—I have been lying down all day
in preparation, you see, Helen—the cool
climate—cool—and the hedges—"

"I see," said Helen, at once, for in sorrow lay this young woman's strength, and a
smile more cheerful than usual came to her
prematurely grave face. "I understand it
all. You have nothing to do now but to
rest."

She went out and despatched one messen-
ger for a doctor, another to her mother, say-

ing she should not be home that night, and
requesting a nursing-gown and certain articles to be sent to her.

The pessimism of Mrs. Herkimer's spirit
may be imagined. "Well, I'm to lose all!
Such fevers are usually ketchin'. Helen was
born in depression, and now she has found
a way to go down the dark valley. Well,
well."

"For God's sake," said the captain, "brace
up! Helen's used to sickness. She's one o'
these 'ere nateral-born Sisters o' Charity.
She's been into everything, and she's come
out all right."

"There's always a last time, Captain Herkimer, and a last straw, and it is fittin', as a
last straw, that the husband of my youth
should go over to Rome!"

"Go over to thunder!" cried the captain.
"Who the devil, then, 's the husband o' your
old age?" And with tears in his eyes, for
his heart was heavy for his only child, he
walked down towards his boat.

He met Judson Sprague on the highway. "Ah, is our Mrs. Stuart with you

this evening, captain, or has she gone home?"

The oily manner irritated the captain. "She's got a bad fever," said he, brusquely, and passed on.

"Ah, too bad! too bad!" said Judson Sprague to the listening atmosphere, and reddened with chagrin and annoyance. The illness of a helpmate, of which he had had considerable experience, was disagreeable to him. Margaret pale and languid was interesting to him. Margaret suffering with a fever was an object, for his own peace of mind, temporarily to be suspended from his affections. "She is, after all, a woman of vigorous constitution. Let us hope she will soon recover—soon recover," he murmured, and retraced his steps homeward.

Overhauling his dory on the beach, the captain saw the Jew strolling near by in the moonlight. He had admired this exponent of an ostracized faith for his skill in Plantagenet's case, and he beckoned to him.

"Would ye like to go out to my boat and take a sail with me? The tide's servin'."

"Thank you, yes," said the Jew, pleasantly.

"I'm all upset to-night," owned the captain, with instant confidence in the other's frank eyes. "Mrs. Stuart, up there, 's in a bad way with a fever, and my Helen's nursin' of her."

"I won't go for the sail, thank you," said Isaac. The captain wondered if some whiter light from the moon had fallen on his face. "I will go up to the house; there may be something I can do."

Helen answered his knock, speaking with him in the hall.

"I thank God you are with her, Miss Herkimer," he said.

The girl read his face, trusted him, and, above all, pitied him.

"You can pull her through! You can save her! Is she suffering? Is she very ill?"

"Yes," said Helen, to this last clause, but with a quiet strength inspired for the emergency.

"When—when—" said the Jew—"when

Mrs. Stuart was well she entrusted this amount to me for safe-keeping. She had business confidence in me." He thrust a roll of bank-notes into Helen's hands. "It is possible she may need them now. She—she had no other confidence in me, though I worship her," said he, as if to a safe confessor in the presence of an awful emergency. "God knows, if I could send her out in health and peace, and myself bear her illness, though to die, I would do it! I hoped—but I seemed always to offend her. I have been much alone. I have not learned the ways of other men. You must pardon me, but she had confidence in my rectitude. The amount is hers. She should have everything done for her—physicians—a nurse to relieve yourself."

Helen, with her steady eyes, divined that the Jew, in this instance, might possibly be a Jesuit of the Jesuits. But his face was a book of pathos, and she did not thwart him.

"I am glad that she has this. It shall be used for her, and I will myself keep the account."

14

"I must not detain you." But Isaac's hand trembled on the baluster with an unfinished appeal.

"Call me by knocking at this outer door whenever you like," said this girl of sad intuitions. "I will come as often as you desire, to tell you how she is."

"God bless you!" said Isaac; and then this legitimate offspring of an unbelieving and acquisitive race went up to Granny's room and laid his head in her lap and cried. Plantagenet and she were saying their prayers on a string of beads. The beads dangled in Isaac's black locks.

"There!" said Granny, gently, at the end, with a face calm as if earthly trouble had never touched her senses; "all is well!"

But Mildred St. Thomas's beads hung gaudily on her beautiful neck, and were not designed for prayer. She, too, came, and Helen went out to her.

"I have come to nurse Mrs. Stuart," said Mildred, with a rather forced boldness in her impressive presence as she confronted her lover's unappreciated fiancée.

If Helen had latterly learned something
of the state of affairs, if she knew that the
splendid beauty before her was implicated
with Jeffrey, she still showed no bitterness
either in her face or voice, and Mildred was
stormily conscious of her own false position.

"If you care for Mrs. Stuart, if you wish
her to live, you will not disturb her now,"
said Helen.

"I—I knew her first."

"Later on, perhaps, you can help us—'Agnes,' as Mrs. Stuart calls her, and me. Later,
perhaps, you can help us."

"Is she so dangerous?"

"She is very ill."

Mildred's hand trembled in the place where
Isaac's had been. She knew persuasion or
rebellion were useless. She went out reck-
lessly, and she prayed *her* prayer — an im-
pious prayer; but she was crude in the effort, and at least it was a beginning.

"O God," said Mildred—popularly known
as Duds Sen' Tammy—" if you will save her
to be in health again, I will join any church
that will take me in — and live up to it! I

will! I don't break my word—you know
that! If not—" the stormy young woman
ground her teeth as in conclusion.

And just at this point the familiar strains
of the Salvation Army suddenly arrested her
on the street. Hundreds of times she had
heard them *without* hearing them, and hundreds of times, in company with Jeffrey, or
some other congenial spirit, she had mocked
their songs or ridiculed their persuasions and
their bonnets.

"Just as I am, without one plea,

\*    \*    \*    \*    \*

O Lamb of God, I come! I come!"

"Just as I am!" Now Mildred was waiting for something—something imperative—
something without which—

"Just as I am!" sang the trumpet, now
without aid of human voice. "Just as I
am! Just as I am!" It filled and flooded
her turbulent brain.

It did not come with any sense of awakened spiritual perceptions to Duds Sen' Tammy. It was a wonder whereat she gasped—

the sudden opening of a new vista on life's common highway, awesome, almost strangely lovely, with undreamed-of possibilities.

It was a natural flood that laved her—a voice piercing to the exclusion of all other voices; and she turned unresistingly and followed the group into their dingy barracks.

## CHAPTER XV

"Here, Plontogonet! Go down to Father
Walsh wid this candle and git it blisséd, till
I burn it for the hilth—God grant it!—o' the
dear one that's ill. Now, I want no progrissions by the way. Mind ye that!"

There was no danger. It was an errand
grateful to the soul of Plantagenet. He carried the candle there and back awesomely in
his soiled, iniquitous hands.

Moral peace now settled upon Mrs. O'Ragan, though her heart was perturbed in many
ways.

"Sure there be fayvers that be light and
some that be hard, Mrs. Shaughnessy!" she
moaned, with doleful suggestion.

"Yis, Mrs. O'Ragan. There's a bit of a
hay-fayver, for insthance, that's little harm
at all."

"Harm, was ye sayin'? 'Tis glad I'd be

to suffer it. Whin we resided in the counthry, six miles beyant, I kipt sivinty hens
and of coos a dizzen and one. Holy Saint
Pather in heaven knows it!"

" I admire yer aristhocracy, Mrs. O'Ragan,
but what has that to do wid yer hay-fayver?"

" Viry much, indade, Mrs. Shaughnessy.
Hay was hay there, and no say-wind a-blas-
thin' it. 'Tis little hay one sees here, grane
or dry."

"True for ye, and the weather grows
blightin'. I seen O'Ragan's shirts ye hung
out yistherday is as sthiff as a ghost, as
though niver a bit o' wather had been wrung
out o' thim."

" Indade, Kate Shaughnessy! Look to your
own drhawers—is flantin' on the line wid the
icicles to thim a yard long!"

" Whish! now—"

Mrs. O'Ragan drew her cable.

Two sleek individuals were coming up the
walk. " We come from the Board of Health;
ladies; merely a little formality."

Mrs. O'Ragan and Mrs. Shaughnessy turned their cannon from one another to sweet,

mutual defence, and a volley of sarcasm
pointed outward.

"Look to yer own Bamboo dwellin's!"
said the dauntless Mrs. O'Ragan.  "Whin I
washed for yer wife, Mr. Capron, sure didn't
I see the maid emp'yin' all the refuge into a
hole forninst the kitchen windy?   Ha! ha!"

Mrs. Shaughnessy also laughed valiantly.

Mr. Capron blushed contemptuously.  "We
have never had a case of severe illness in our
house, madam."

"No, and ye're not a poor soul, overborne
wid trial and misfortin', that was daintily
r'ared, like the poor sick lady that's higher
borned than iver ye had any dr'amin' of;
but whin she's ill, ye must come here nosin'
around to find the cause of it in a bit of
orange-pale in the coort-yard or a mug o'
stale milk on me panthry shilf!   Do ye make
yer girdle-cakes o' swate milk, then?   God
knows when I ate them to your house, I
thought I was 'atin' the soles off me own
shoes!   Ha! ha!"

"Ha! ha!" echoed Mrs. Shaughnessy, with
delirious scorn.

"But come in; the law sint ye. Come in and smill! From the odors I met wid in yer own risidence it will be a pleasant change to ye; and I don't begrudge yer eyes for onct from dwellin' on a clane staircase!"

Mrs. Shaughnessy, absorbed in admiration of her general, gave a rapturous giggle.

"Come in! Come in and smill—do!" repeated Mrs. O'Ragan.

Very haughtily the two gentlemen inspected the place and premises. "There may be no direct cause of fever here, madam, but the general appearance is unkempt and shackling. Look at that old broom, for instance, leaning against the outside of the house."

"Look at it!" said Mrs. O'Ragan, folding her arms, her cable taut—"look at it! wid a bit of a white rag tied to it for dark nights! Look at it! but tech it wid a point o' yer finger, and I'll saze it and lay it over the Bamboo o' the two o' ye! Begone!"

"I've been told she's a vixen," said one inspector to the other, not taking the pains to make the remark inaudible to its subject.

Mrs. O'Ragan, with folded arms of full contempt, watched them out of sight. She then leaned her head over on Mrs. Shaughnessy and wept.

"The dear, swate lady! I feel it in my sowl 'tis goin' hard wid her. Me heart's clane broke, Katie, dear. The house is goin' disthracted, and mesilf wid it, sinct she was taken ill."

Mrs. Shaughnessy bore her commander soothingly on her breast.

"'Tis one o' yer own family, Bridget, and the swatest, and it's tearin' the poor gizzard out o' ye. Maybe ye nade a drhop o' somethin' sustainin'."

"I detist the sight o' it," said Mrs. O'Ragan, "but maybe 'twill keep me up to perform me duties and drowned me sorrows. Don't be seen in the dram-shop, Katie—'tis not ilegant — but get it off the sody man, and tell him 'tis wanted only physical. Mind the word, Katie — get it physical."

Readily Mrs. Shaughnessy threw the fringe of her shawl over her head and

stalked her tall and slender person jauntily
to the druggist's.

"A quart of it, physical," said she.

"A quart of what? if you please, madam."

"Oh, get away wid ye!" said Mrs. Shaughnessy, who had been something of a flirt in
her day; and she winked—the technicali-
ties of commonplace existence not being unknown to her either.

"What quality will you have, madam?"

"Ye didn't know, did ye!" the lady airily
rated him. "Sure, your best physical," and
with her parcel under her arm, she returned
to her fellow-wrestler in life's Olympic ring.

Now Mrs. O'Ragan and Mrs. Shaughnessy
never got drunk; it was seldom, and only
under circumstances of peculiar distress, that
they imbibed at all, and when they did so,
it was by table-spoonfuls at regular inter-
vals, that sustained Mrs. O'Ragan in a condition gloomily intrepid and kept her lighter-
witted companion trippingly elate. Under
this stimulus, however, duties even out of
the ordinary round now appealed to them.

" 'Tis a long time since the cats has had a dose o' catnip, Bridget. We would not be havin' the poor cr'atures in fits."

" True. Catch them and bring them in to me, Katie, while I'm puttin' the 'arb to draw."

This injunction Mrs. Shaughnessy proceeded to obey, with a perkish impartiality of detail grabbing one cat after another off the fence, where they lay sunning in an apparently interminable line. Mrs. O'Ragan, with a solemnity as methodical, dosed them and returned them to the world of nature.

At last Mrs. Shaughnessy brought in a cat with what had once been a beautiful ribbon round its neck, and at sight of it Mrs. O'Ragan threw up her spoon wildly, overturning the dish of catnip on the stove, and buried her face in her hands.

" 'Tis *her* kitten! Oh, me! oh, me!"

Mrs. Shaughnessy purged a spoonful of tea from the streaming mixture on the stove, administered it to the cat with an unceremonious dismissal, and then put *her* head down and began to weep, her mercurial sympathies

flowing as readily in tears as in mirth. Thus
Plantagenet found them and regarded them
with hopeful curiosity.

"Plontogonct," said Mrs. O'Ragan, "yer
mother's weery, me child. Will yez black
the stove for her?"

The boy's eyes shone. Left alone in the
room, he first polished the stove energetically, then decided to take it to pieces and put
it together again — a thing that had long
been one of the minor objects of his ambi-
tion. He was a strong lad, and he was suc-
ceeding admirably in the process of dissec-
tion, when, as though he had touched the
main-spring or combination key in some
subtle joint, the whole structure, preluded
by the frying-pans, and consummated by
the stove-pipe, fell over him on the floor.
Extricating himself, he fled with a few
bounds to Sanctuary.

It was Saturday evening, and O'Ragan
himself, coming home with a bit of comfort
in his pocket, scented a general air of concession to human frailties in the house—an
infringement on the decorous conservatism of

manner which had prevailed since the fine
lady came to dwell among them. He sighed
and patiently put up the stove.

Both Mrs. O'Ragan and Mrs. Shaughnessy
commended him. " 'Tis a good man I have,
Katie. Heaven grant I'll niver see no insurance on him! Sure I'd be flingin' it back in
the face o' them for an insoolt that 'u'd go
offerin' me insurance on me man—the poor,
patient cr'atur'!"

" He is that!" replied Mrs. Shaughnessy ;
"and a mate for me own, that's got an as-
surance on him, too; but let anybody come
offerin' that same to me, he'd think 'twas the
expriss had struck 'm! If there's anything
more to say," added Mrs. Shaughnessy, " me
fists shall say it!"

" Beautiful women desarves good husban's," said O'Ragan, who had taken a sip
of refreshment while at work. He, indeed,
had been originally a handsome man, and he
now rose and bowed low.

Mrs. O'Ragan put her apron to her eyes
with painful pleasure. Mrs. Shaughnessy
laughed coquettishly.

"Rose of Killarney!" said O'Ragan, bowing low before his wife, "will ye h'ist a step o' the ould dance wid me?"

Mrs. O'Ragan's pessimism — unlike Mrs. Herkimer's—was always valiant. She rose and courtesied with a melodramatic sweep of her draperies.

"Wait ti' I get Jamie!" said Mrs. Shaughnessy, "and we'll have the 'Peeler's Reel,' wid the windy open for a revivin' breath on us."

With Jamie came others, male and female, buoyed up by the trifling elation incident to a week well ended. Plantagenet ventured down and found his obliquities lost, like dry leaves, far down the winds of oblivion. Delightedly he went out and tacked a placard over the sentinel broom:

*CIRKUS IN HERE!!*
*GOTES A DIME,*
*KIDS A NICKKIL.*

After a markedly decorous dance the occupants of the kitchen sat down and reflected with acute sympathy the stanchly sorrowful countenance of their hostess. She whispered to her husband. "I move," said he, gallantly, "that a conthribution be taken up for the ilegant lady in misfortin' that's sick above-stairs."

With the natural air of a lord, he emptied all the money that was his by Saturday-night possession into the hat; he literally cleaned out his pockets, and joy without compunction shone on his features as he passed the receptacle on. A like example of voluptuous giving was shown on every side. The sum—and it was not an inconsiderable one—was handed to Mrs. O'Ragan, and she toiled up-stairs with it, her heart beating for joy.

Helen came out.

"'Tis a bit of remimbrance among us, darlin', remimbrin' the kindness and love of the dear one that's afflicthed," and she emptied the sum with trembling haste and turned to retreat.

"Stop!" said Helen. "Stop! Mrs. O'Ragan." Catholics and Jews and what not! And the girl had been trained in rigorous distrust of them all. But Helen was an intuitive scholar, and the tears swam in her eyes and her cheeks were flushed with a feeling that was not indignation. "Stop!" said she, pressing the money back into Mrs. O'Ragan's hands; "when she is able she shall know of your lovely kindness. But she does not need this—she has more than sufficient—she had something reserved in a case of need like this. Thank you, with all my heart! Thank you all!"

Mrs. O'Ragan returned, explained, and redistributed the money.

"'Tis swately she done it," said she. "Sure 'tis a Bamboo she is, but steppin' handy on the idge o' convarsion, and puggeratory niver 'll contain her lang, mark me words to that!"

The distributants took back their cash, not as cheerfully as it had been given, but with philosophy.

"Well thin, God be thanked!" said they.

Isaac, coming home, saw the sign posted over the sentinel broom, and withdrew it, his sombre eyes lighting only with a sort of

15

fatherly compassion for the vagabond Plantagenet. He called him, and the sad one appeared. Plantagenet now, whether involved
in crime, in debt, or in affection, equally
trusted the Jew.

"Is that a nice thing to have posted on
the house, when a lady of the Stuarts is
lying ill, think you?"

"I didn' mean to! I don' care what hap-
pens—the heart o' me's clane broke in me!"
said Plantagenet, accepting his mother's language in his desperation, and laying his head
in his ragged sleeve.

## CHAPTER XVI

In a room that Helen kept chaste and quiet from all the small turmoils of life, Margaret rambled on through a fever as weary and capricious as if the pulse of life were maimed and could never take up its normal course again. Strange vagaries absorbed her fitfully, and might have entertained one with a keener sense of humor than Helen Herkimer; but Helen took all with careful seriousness, weighed these swallow flights, and returned them with just appreciation and a smile of constant loyalty. Possibly, this gravity of manner helped Margaret back to the gravity of existence. Agnes, no less tender, giggled unguardedly now and then.

"Sister," said Margaret, "you are good, but in this present ex—ex—" said the sick one, laying her hand on her head for her vagrant list of long words—" I need, besides you, a *Catholic*, a true Catholic."

" So? Dear Miz' Stuart, God shall bless you! I am doze all ovaire!" cried Agnes, cheerfully.

" But I need," said Margaret, with her large eyes solemn and exalted to the occasion, " one who has taken vows—like this one!" She touched Helen reverently with her thin hand.

Helen blushed painfully. Here was a jagged problem indeed.

Agnes regarded the situation with broad optimism.

" I will go look after my boys one while now," she said; " then I shall relief you."

Margaret heard the door close, and pondered deeply what she would next say.

" I would not talk," said Helen, with the utmost gentleness. " I would not talk now."

" I must. As the saint—angel—God sent to me, will you—you—take my trouble and con—condition and all off of me and bear them—till I know how to do so? Now, will you?"

Helen met frankly the compelling intentness of the other's look.

" Christ will do that," she said, slowly.

" Very — very true," was the response, startling in a naked simplicity of logic; "but I do not see Him, and I see you. Now, will you ?"

Margaret, in health, had a way of putting her soul into her eyes, and now they regarded Helen as though life itself hung on the solution of the theme propounded.

Helen turned very pale; the fountains of her orthodoxy were stirred. Impiety—profanity itself—stared her in the face.

The dilemma suited the recumbent one; she had a grateful sense that she was still up to the discussion of metaphysical subtleties, and that Helen would take no vantage ground.

Helen watched the shadow of a hand trembling on the coverlet. The doctor had said a day would decide the fever's turn now. It was no time for ecclesiastical logic or excitement. She closed her eyes with an inaudible " Forgive me!" and let her orthodoxy slip to the winds.

"Yes, I will," she said, with the usual careful decision, and a smile even more than usually reassuring.

Margaret sank back as though the mountains had been rolled off of her, slept and slept, and woke, feeble, but autocratically sane. " When can I see Mildred?" she said. " I am anxious about Plantagenet. I would like to see—" the pinched face flushed. " Please hand me my porridge, Helen. I get nothing to eat!"

Now Helen's rival, in her crude way, had been growing into and putting on something of the regalia of saintship too. Truth to tell, Mildred had never once admired herself in her " Salvation" bonnet; her thoughts had turned another way, like the straight flight of a bird. Nevertheless, her alluring features had never been framed in anything so becoming.

Jeff protested, while admiring.

" Well, wear what you like, do what you like—only you're not going to shift *me* off; you are not going to get so good that you

want to do that. I'll throttle you first!"
Jeff laughed, but with considerable excitement.

Mildred had made up her mind to something. It cut her at every word she uttered, like the sapping of a young tree, but she did not flinch.

"Helen Herkimer is a saint, Jeff; she'd give her life for anybody! She'll never be put out of her rights by me!"

"What do you mean? If you think you'll turn me back to Helen with that kind of talk, you will see!" he threatened, harshly. "Helen is all right, but she's nothing to me."

"Well, then," said Mildred, with another swift decision, "I care more for somebody else, Jeff," and she wet her lips and drew her breath as though she had just gathered herself up from a blow. "If I tell him," she thought, "that it is to do the Only Right, though it kills me, and that it is my Lord Saviour I love best, he will laugh and wait; he will never leave off—so this settles it. Some time, maybe—he'll know."

So Mildred, too, trod the Jesuitical path, with a bleeding heart of self-sacrifice at least.

Jeff's shock head seemed stunned; his own lips grew thin and parched.

"Somebody down at the Salvation Army?" he said, mechanically.

"Yes," said Mildred, "it's Somebody down at the Salvation Army. (Some time, perhaps, he'll know—he'll know.)"

"Well, by God! Helen's *faithful*, anyway!" sneered the young fellow in a high voice. Quivering, and without another word, he turned and walked away.

Mildred crawled home like a broken thing. "But it's right — it's right! It's got to be borne! Oh, Jeff! Oh, my boy! my boy!—

> "'Saviour, more than life to me,
> I am clinging, clinging'"—

this special Salvationist's voice, usually so confident and clear, sounded more now like a spent old woman's as she climbed up the lodging stairs—

> "'close to Thee.
> Trusting Thee, I shall not stray.
> I shall never—never—lose my way.
> Never—never'"—

sobbed the voice, low and brokenly—

> "'lose my way.'"

"Miss Sen' Tammy," said the landlady, "they've sent down word to ye; ye can come see the lady ye've been frettin' over. She's not dangerous any more."

"Thank you, yes, I'm going. 'Never, never,'" the voice clung persistently to the strain, "'lose-my-way.'"

Having brushed her hair into the austere form she had adopted, and from which it was ever in a gay quarrel to escape, Mildred, with a gentle and cautious touch, took from among her belongings the white dress Margaret had given her, and as quietly unfolded it.

"I think, to please her," she whispered to herself, "I'll wear the white dress; I've never had it on. Yes, I think, to please her,

I'll wear it. I sha'n't be proud," she gasped, " nor take back Jeff. I see the way. I'm going to walk it. And I think, to please her, I can put it on now.

"'Never—never—lose—my—way.'"

Thus arrayed, Mildred turned away from the glass, cold to the vivid charms reflected there. This unbaptized vagrant of the canning factory had a stout heart when she "saw the way" and realized in her simple faith once more a capacity for the old feat of martyrdom.

Jeff saw her pass, glowering from a shop-window, where he was buying a new tie for some purpose. Fine cords drew and pinched his heart at that radiant vision, but he set his teeth and turned to a higher brilliancy in his selection of color.

"If she thinks she can throw me off as light as an old shoe, and watch me suffer, she's mistaken! I'll go make merry with Helen—that is, as merry as one can."

Margaret read a clear story when Mildred came in—Helen, too. But the girl chatted

away of bits of pleasant news, and how fast
Margaret was gaining, and she heard the
doctor had said "'twas Helen Herkimer that
saved her."

Helen was regarding the girl with the
wonder of a new conviction.

"And you are working in the same
place?" said Margaret.

"Yes, there, and in the Army."

"Oh yes, I know! I know!" said Margaret, as if she had been told. "Do you *work*
in the Army?"

"I should think so!" Mildred, laughing,
held up her hands in confirmation. "We
look them up, we scrub and wash and nurse
and sew. Yes, I should think so. Why,
there'd be no life in it if you did not work!"

"When I am stronger," said the Stuart,
holding the girl's hands at leave-taking, "I
want to learn some things of you. I know!
I know! darling."

Mildred blushed with a quick joy. "I
am going away," she bent and whispered—
"a long way off. It will be best for Jeff—
and all. I am going to work in the place

where my aunt lives. There's work there
and the Army just the same."

"I know! I know," said Margaret, still as
if she had been told. But she clung to the
girl's hand.

Mildred seemed the older, with that strong
peace on her face as she stooped to Margaret.

"I shall have you always," she said—"always. And some time I shall have you
where people don't get wrenched apart."
And at that she kissed her as if there were
need of haste, for people had a way of loving Margaret not appreciable except in the
fact itself.

Mildred went home and laid the white
dress away. "There's another time when
I'll wear it," she said; and the broken-
hearted girl was thinking of that "Lover
down at the Salvation Army," the tryst
with Whom is kept only by the fording of a
certain cold stream.

Plantagenet and Isaac knew that their
lady had been receiving a friend or two, and,
under the disguise of talking about bait for

"pog" fishing, they comforted the turbulence of one another's hearts in the front yard.

"Plontojonay! Plontojonay!" called Agnes, from the window, "Miz' Stuart say she see you one meenet!"

Plantagenet was indeed already brushed and in his best, but now he fell a-trembling. He caught up with Tommy Sullivan on the stairs. Tommy, always eating bread and treacle, was as broad as he was long. Too indifferent for more active service in the "Kore," he had been deputed to priestly office and had been given a name from Plantagenet's own book of history.

"Come 'long, Leggit," said the trembling commander-in-chief. "I want you to come 'long with me!"

Tommy, his hands dripping sweetness, had no objection to disseminating it further—indeed, he rather affected progression. Plantagenet thrust him first into the room.

"I thought you might like to see this little chub," he gasped, obviously seeking to hide his own perturbation. "He's 'Leggit of the 'Postolic See.'"

The Legate of the Apostolic See took a
bite from the overflowing gifts of Providence,
and gazed with indifferent and general interest about the room.

At the sight Margaret laughed as though
the world had come back to her.

" And you, Plantagenet, why do you not
come up and speak to me?"

Plantagenet had a look holier than when
he carried the candles.  He stepped stiffly towards Margaret's bedside.  "How de do?" he
said.  But at the touch of her hand he choked.

"Why, my little boy!" she said, and drew
his face down; and at that this poor Irish
vagabond and great living representative of
the Stuarts fell a-sobbing.

"What is the matter?"—Isaac waited for
him below—"is she worse?"

"No, no," said Plantagenet, growing stout
at the sight of one even more sentimental
than himself; "no, sir; she's boss."

"What are you crying about?"

"Why, she—she kisst me! and she whispert to me, too!"

" Did she ask—about any of us ?"

" She whispert me ef you was well."

" No!"

" Yes, sir—she did ; and I—I said you was
thinner 'n an old sea-quail wi' worritin' about
her !"

" Honor bright, Plantagenet ?"    Isaac was
trembling now.

" Honor bright !"    Plantagenet's beautiful
eyes were lifted, unassailable, with the heart-
broken truth.

" Let's go down-town, Plantagenet."

" See here," said Isaac, pausing before a
shop-window, " you've worn a navy cap so
long now you are really commander of a land
force, you know !    What do you say to that
major - general's cap in there with the gilt
bands ?"

" She's none too much for me !" said Plantagenet.    And, in truth, the cap was none
too great for him.

" Them pink sodys look nice in there,
don't they ?"    Plantagenet suggested, as they
moved on.

" Why, to be sure !    What flavor is that ?

Strawberry? Ah, that's good! that's good!
Come, we'll go in! We must brace up, my
boy, for we've some shopping to do yet!"

And the treasures with which Plantagenet
returned home after that memorable walk
occupied rapturous days for himself and
Granny in Sanctuary.

## CHAPTER XVII

JEFF took the first opportunity of Helen's partial return to her home to present himself.

Helen had never seen him look so much like his father. He had gotten himself up, face and all, for a hypocrite, only whereas the father was smooth, the son was an ill one; and the torment produced in the piercing of his swart neck by an immaculate new collar showed in undisguised anguish on his face.

"I am glad, Helen," he began, "that you have been so good to Mrs. Stuart. I am very fond of her myself. We are all very fond of her. I wish that she would marry my father. Do you think"—Jeff saw with horror that his kid glove had split at the thumb. He concealed the rent with a flurried attempt at secrecy—"do you think that she will ever marry my father?"

16

"I am very sure, Jeff, that she will never marry your father."

"No, I should think not," said Jeff, throwing his arms out and letting his fine raiment strain and creak as it liked. "We are to be trifled with and thrown over and snubbed! That is what we are for!"

"Jeffrey," said Helen, meeting his anger with a pair of dark eyes, kind, but not easy to get away from, "has anybody snubbed you?"

Jeff fairly perspired in this dilemma.

"You are snubbing me now by looking at me as though I were a beast."

"You do not seem to me like a beast at all, Jeff. You seem to me like an honest fellow, who has something on his heart to tell me."

"I al—always loved you, Helen," responded the faithless Jeff, with tears; "but she was so loud and jolly and—handsome!"

"Mildred?"

"Yes—the hussy! She's run off and gone to the bad with another fellow! Serves her right!"

"I will tell you what she did. She is a noble girl—Mildred St. Thomas is. She has not run off with any man at all. She has given herself to be good and true and to help others, and she left you of her own resolve, because it seemed to her a duty."

"She told me she liked somebody else better."

"She meant the very highest devotion of all, Jeff."

"Oh—guns!" said Jeff, whose spiritual perceptions still hardly attained to the primary form. "I beg your pardon, Helen—I mean—oh—"

"And if you love her truly, you would better try to walk the same path she is going so bravely in, and then you might meet some time and be worthy of one another. I do not think, as it was, you would have helped one another. But now—"

Jeff's jaw fell. Helen, calmly giving him away, had never looked so charming. Helen's black hair waved amazingly prettily, and how small and dainty her ears were! and such a proud, tantalizing, womanly smile!

Jeff leaped up. "Do you think I would
marry anybody, Helen Herkimer, that went
gaping around the streets in a poke-bonnet,
yelling, and shaking a drum-head with a
fringe of bells round it! Well, you *have* an
opinion of me! Ha! ha!" He took a
righteously injured attitude.

Helen's eyes dwelt on him with some contempt. He melted and fell.

"I'm a good-for-nothing ass," said he.
"I'm going out to drown myself."

"I would be a man, with God's help, first!"
said Helen. "It would be kinder to those
you leave."

"But you don't love me any more. Oh,
Helen!" Jeff, with unpremeditated tragedy,
knelt before her and laid his pitiable head on
her knee. "I do love you! I love you more
than I ever loved, or ever could love, any
other woman. Oh, Helen, I'll be all that you
wish, if you'll only have me!"

Helen's slender fingers did not run into
his hair as they had done in days of blessed
memory so perilously lost. He waited in
vain.

"Oh, Helen!"

She gently pushed him up and away from her. What a grave, beautiful, womanly face she had!

"You cannot prove it to me by any words, Jeff. You can only prove it by time and your own actions."

"I *will* prove it!"

"Very well." She was moving away.

"Oh, Helen!"

She was gone.

Jeff stood like a statue, pale and pondering.

"Well, Jeffrey," said Mrs. Herkimer, observing him as she swept into the room, "I see you have caught the family depression."

"If I could catch anything of Helen," said Jeff, "I'd take it and die of it with pleasure."

"I must say, Jeffrey, I should prefer to choose my own disease, and not go into everything, hit or miss, as Helen does."

"She may go into all the diseases she likes, Mrs. Herkimer, and I'll go with her and help her to the best of my poor, poor ability, if she'll only let me!"

Mrs. Herkimer's attention by this time had become more closely fixed.

"You've experienced a change, perhaps, Jeffrey?" she said, with a soothing air of sectarian hopefulness.

"Yes, yes," said the materially minded Jeff, with wild regret; "I experienced a change, Mrs. Herkimer, but I'm all over it, thank God, forever!"

"Well, well"—gasped Mrs. Herkimer—"well, Jeffrey, harder cases have been broken by the anvil of the rock."

"No anvil is ever going to break me up again, Mrs. Herkimer."

"Poor Helen!" sighed the lady. "Well, she courts obdurit cases, and—"

"Oh, if she'll only ever court me," cried Jeff, "or let me court her!"

"Oh," said Mrs. Herkimer, freshly adjusting her glasses, "I perceive! You are arguing from a fleshly stan'point, Jeffrey?"

The captain laughed as he came in with his newspaper. "Well, Nell, what stan'point are you arguin' from? Ye weigh a han'some hunderd and eighty, God bless ye! I wouldn't have ye a mite less."

"If I haven't pined, Captain Herkimer," replied his lady, sententiously, " it hasn't been for lack o' trials."

" Ye fatten on 'em, Nell — ye fatten on 'em !" said the captain, bravely, gloating over the first page of his paper. " God bless ye, Nell—ye fatten on 'em !"

"Captain Herkimer, here is a youth who is in a frame that, if he might be spoken to by one who had not hidden his light under a bushel—"

"Say an oat-bin, Nell—I'm a little broader 'n that—come, say an oat-bin !"

" Under a bushel—"

The captain looked up gravely at Jeff from over his newspaper. " Ye are in a frame, ain't ye, my boy?" he said, kind and comprehensive sympathy in his eyes, and scanning Jeff's tight new trousers and lacerated gloves. " Go and take off them togs, Jeff ! What is a strong young fellow like you doin' around in broad daylight with yer legs pinioned and yer hands in a lot o' lilac rags? Go home and get on some clo'es, my son, and go to work! Ye'll find what 'salvation' means then. Go to work and make yer way—it's in ye—go to work, my son!"

Jeff's intelligence was touched at last, and his heart. ("My son!") He went over and grasped the captain's hand.

"I'll prove worthy of Helen, captain. I will!" he said.

"Men," said Mrs. Herkimer, "are all alike. And yet there's a pernicious sect in this town that's rabblin' to be saved on their own merits!"

She sighed, wholesomely.

## CHAPTER XVIII

Mrs. Herkimer had vigorous champions in this thought that she wot not of.

Mrs. O'Ragan and Mrs. Shaughnessy, approaching the dregs of that draught which was purely physical, decided to make an end, and subsequently reached a condition even of irascibility on ethical grounds.

"'Tis two dizzen can'les me own poor silf has offered for the dear lady's hilth—and hilth it is is lightin' in her swate, big, voylet eyes again, God be thanked!"

"One dizzen have I."

"And yit there's some niver burns a can'le, Katie—no, niver a one!"

Mrs. Shaughnessy shook her head inexpressibly.

"And yit," continued Mrs. O'Ragan, "d' ye hear. This very avenin' their haythen Bamboo bells is ringin' in me ears."

"I darst ye to go in at them, Bridget."

"Well do ye know, Katie," said Mrs. O'Ragan, rising with resignation, "no Stuart ever swallys a thrit. I've a sevare cabbage thirst on me," she interpolated. "I'll stop in at the grane grocer's and selict a blossom o' the same agin to-morry's pot."

"Would it be well to sphrinkle ourselves a bit, Bridget, considerin' of where we're goin'?"

"Ye're not the only one to have the thought, Katie. Bring the holy wather."

Mrs. Shaughnessy, in some confusion of choice, brought the bottle of benzoin; and fragrantly they departed.

Where, before, the suffering ornamental bird in Mrs. O'Ragan's bonnet had held a peanut in its tottering beak, Plantagenet had lately inserted a very old and forlorn ginger-cookie, and, for further security, had not disdained the use of an effete shoestring in clinching it in position.

Unconsciously, and with an almost paralyzing dignity, Mrs. O'Ragan sailed forth.

Mrs. Shaughnessy, too, to give loftier disapprobation to her demeanor, had cocked her "Darby" hat on one side.

As they flowed into the unsuspecting group at the doors, they had an unmistakable air of wishing somebody to attack them. Though there was no crowd, least of all about the pungently anointed persons of these two, Mrs. O'Ragan chose to believe that she was pressed.

"What the ding's the matter o' ye here?" she exclaimed, valiantly working her elbows in clear space. "I'll see whether a poor Irishwoman is goin' to be flattened forninst the wall be a lot o' unbelavin' Bamboos!"

Mrs. Shaughnessy confirmed this challenge with a laugh of startling irony.

And all the while it looked as though the whole innocent force of heresy combined could hardly have flattened Mrs. O'Ragan's encabled form against the wall.

"I'm like that old haythen, Cram'll," she continued, drawing on Plantagenet's history, and addressing her amazed and inoffensive foe-at-large—"I'm like that old haythen, Cram'll, begorry!—I niver counts me inimy!"

"No, niver," said Katie, "nor me—no, not a one!"

And still no combatant stepped forth in active opposition. The utmost largess of environment was also allowed them in their selection of seats, and of this they availed themselves, each occupying the centre of a form, with arms high-folded, and a posture the most distinctly inimical.

A rather pleasantly argumentative and familiar discourse was being delivered from the platform, to which the fraternity now and then responded with a cheerful "Amen!"

But Mrs. O'Ragan's spirit had by this time reached the trumpet-call for the onset.

"Amin! Amin! Amin!" she exclaimed, scornfully aloud, and very much aloud. "Amin foriver and yit niver stoppin'! Amin! and Amin! and yit goin' on wid it always the same! Ha! ha!"

"Ha! ha!" thrillingly echoed Katie.

"Ladies," said a benevolent-looking gentleman, softly approaching them at this juncture, "allow me to escort you to the door."

His manner was so bland that Katie's vola-

tile nature instantly acquiesced, wearied beside with the heat and the uncongenial aspect
of the place.

"Sure, yes," said she, alertly; "we'll be
goin'. Ye must excuse us. We only came
in by r'ason of feelin' a bit playful."

"Sure, yes," said Mrs. O'Ragan, grimly,
and glad at heart to forsake the field; "'tis
amusement intirely we came for."

"You have both received and given it.
Are these your groceries, madam?" continued the urbane individual, overtaking Mrs.
O'Ragan in the aisle and courteously hand-
ing her the unveiled cabbage, which she had
purchased by the way and frankly deposited
on the seat beside her.

"There now!" exclaimed Mrs. O'Ragan,
enabled by this rencounter to depart amid
the dying clash of arms in bannered victory—
"there now! a poor Irishwoman can't come
in among ye widout havin' the viry cabbage
stoled off her! And so it is—Bamboo, indade!—that a poor hard-workin' woman
can't come in here widout ye'd be stalin' the
viry cabbage off her! Ah, so, indade!"

And in this high tone, with supplementary murmurings of indignation from Katie, they withdrew, as it were, enlaurelled.

But at home, after the cool walk, Mrs. O'Ragan fell a-sobbing.

"Oh, Katie, what have I done?—me, a respickkable woman! Whatever was in me? Shame to me, Katie! shame to me!"

"'Tis a bit fayverish ye are, Bridget darlin'! Sure, 'twas no harm done."

"Oh, Katie, 'tis many a pinance I'll do mysilf on this night's ja'ntin'! 'Tis well I served my Lord this night! Oh, shame on me!" and fell again a-bemoaning.

So sincere and lamentable was her state, Katie, too, sank, pierced by contrition, and their tears mingled.

"'Tis a fine lesson I've showed them poor wand'rin' Bamboos this night! Ah, fine! Shame to me! And there's many a good Bamboo, Katie!"

"There is so, Bridget. Look at Hillen Harkimer, that nursed the dear lady night and day!"

At this specific arrow of recollection, Mrs.

O'Ragan groaned aloud with such material
and voiceful groans a fellow-tenant put her
head in at the door.

"Can I be borryin' a few coals off ye, Mrs.
O'Ragan, ma'am, till the mornin'?" she sub-
mitted, seeing that Mrs. O'Ragan's spirit was
still firmly implanted in her flesh.

"Yis, and wilcome! wilcome!" said Mrs.
O'Ragan, with relief. "Our blisséd Master
tills us to lind."

"I couldn't take them from ye, ma'am,"
said the interloper, struck by the other's
manner of passionate generosity, "widout
ye'd be promisin' to take them back again."

"Oh, nivir fear!" interposed Katie, with
supreme pertness. "It's glad enough anybody'd be to get the return of a loan off ye,
Nora. Sure, I've sometimes thought if I had
a porious plaster on me chist ye'd be borryin' it off me back!"

"Kate Shaughnessy!" said Mrs. O'Ragan,
in clear reproof, and she rose solemnly to
perform her own penances.

She loaned here and she loaned there, hop-
ing for nothing again. And, with a cabbage

thirst⁻ on her, she deliberately gave away that choice flower of many perils to a family with a similar chronic craving and poorer than herself.  And the next morning she walked a mile to procure a particular bit of tenderloin.

"I'll brile it for her, the way the fine folks diz," she said.  "Though for mesilf, I like it me own way best; but maybe 'tis not fine enough for the likes o' her."

She carried it up to Margaret.  Margaret tasted, then looked up with that singular gift of the eyes prone in infatuating humanity.

"I would rather have had it," she said, with adorable fretfulness, "in your old way —dressed with an onion."

Mrs. O'Ragan went down the stairs as if she trod on air.

"'Tis your middlin' class is hard to get along wid," she affirmed; "the old aristhocracy o' the Stuarts is as aisy as yer shoe, every time!"

## CHAPTER XIX

HELEN still spent the greater part of each day at the tenements with Margaret.

As soon as the Stuart began to weigh things reasonably again she drew a very natural sigh.

"I must be vastly in debt—in debt not only for heavenly and unspeakable kindness, but very sordidly so in many directions as well."

Helen meditated a moment, then she spoke with grave composure.

"You must have forgotten the sum you intrusted to the care of Mr. Gilchrist. It has been more than enough."

Margaret gazed point-blank at her companion with blazing eyes. Helen did not lift her calm face from her book.

"Pardon me; you must be reading something very interesting," said the Stuart, coldly, at last.

17

"Let me read you this chapter," suggested the young Jesuit with ready animation, and she began.

"Don't!" Margaret interrupted her, petulantly. "I never had the fortitude to be read aloud to in my best estate, and I am not strong yet—you know I am not strong," the haughty voice broke pitifully and the eyes were unsafe to look at. Helen longed to rush to her, but she only stopped reading aloud and bent stoically to her book.

The next time her attention was arrested by the Stuart that lady had collected herself, and she gave a wicked laugh.

"Helen, however valuable may be the practical lessons in which you are absorbed in that volume, I stand, or, rather, recline, before you as a living example, which please regard — a living example of worldly prudence and foresight. Please look up at me, Helen. Do you not think it was wise of me to be so provident?" The voice was as treacherous as a sigh.

Helen looked up and met those laughing, slumberously revengeful, beautiful eyes.

" I think—" she cried, warmly and bluntly
—" I care not whether he is a Jew or what he
is—I think Mr. Gilchrist is as honest and—
splendid, and true a man as ever lived!
There!"

" Why, assuredly, my dear. Do you think
I should have put funds, so important to me,
in his care, if I had not believed him to be
that ?"

" Oh, but you are laughing in your heart,
and you are cruel. Oh, Mrs. Stuart, if you
only knew!" Helen, rose-red with emotion,
looked ready to cry.

" But why all this tragedy, Helen? I
asked you a simple question, and you have
not answered it. Now do not you think I
was very provident?"

Helen gave the other a compendiously reproachful glance, and bent, scarlet, to the
printed page.

" Oh, Helen, always have something committed to the brokers—how much I cannot
advise exactly, as my illness seems to have
obliterated from my mind the precise extent
of my own most fortunate deposit; but the

example holds good, and you have admitted that I stand, or, rather, recline, before you as a shining light."

Helen did not look up until she began to wonder at Margaret's quietness; then she saw that she had both arms laid across her eyes.

She went to her and spoke. Margaret did not answer. She lifted the arms and found a white face, tear-washed, as if it had been smitten, over and over, by waves of suffering.

"Oh, darling!" said the girl, with an impulse to throw her own soul before the woman in penitence without reason and in adoring caresses, when a truer thought came to her. "You have no trust even in what is most worth trusting," she sighed, gently; "you have no faith in any one, I think."

CHAPTER XX

But the Stuart's proud soul, withal, had
been beaten as with whips, and was lethar-
gic in despair.

"Come out just for a bit of a walk," Hel-
en urged, another day. "The doctor said
you might. The day is perfect."

"Wait till to-morrow, dear," replied Margaret, with insinuating readiness. "I will
try to go to-morrow. But I am so desperately *tired*. So, as I was telling you—" She
went on with some pretty reminiscence.

"But you would gain so much faster if
you only *wished* to gain," interposed Helen,
"and if you would come out."

"Surely, yes; I must try to-morrow. You
are a wise little woman."

Helen looked at the proud, sweet-featured
face, smilingly suave, even in the extremity
of its hopelessness.

"Come, dear Mrs. Stuart, just come to the window! See! the sky is like June."

"Is it? Ah, so it is, I think." Margaret looked up very listlessly. "And, as I was telling you, dear—" She resumed her story, playing with the curtain tassel, when Isaac Gilchrist was seen suddenly approaching up the walk.

Margaret dropped her toy as if she had been given a blow. But Isaac never raised his eyes. And herein had Margaret so re-assuring a confidence that he would not raise his eyes that she still stood at the window, and they watched him enter the door.

"Is not he good?" said the Stuart, with a touch of animation.

"He is very good, indeed, I think," replied Helen, rather bitterly. "He longs very much to see you," she added.

"Why, to be sure; he is such an inestima-ble friend, Helen," said the lady, with amaz-ingly oblivious composure. "But I am not able yet—I really am not able."

Helen looked too unwarily into the infatuating despair of the Stuart's eyes, and temporarily deserted her guns.

"No, I think you are not able yet," she murmured. So she prepared Margaret's supper, sat with her a little longer, and left her, as was her wont now, for the night.

Margaret slept after her illness weakly, absolutely like a child.

But in the middle of this night her frail door was shaken, then crashed in. She woke in a nightmare of smoke and crackling flames.

"Where is your dressing-gown?" gasped Isaac Gilchrist. "Here! Quick!"

"I cannot see!" she cried, half-way across the room, and hid her eyes in pain against his coat. He lifted and carried her.

So at midnight they stood as in the heat and glow of an awful noonday by the poplar-tree at the gate.

"Why are they putting up the ladder?" said Margaret. "The people are all out, surely? See!"

Isaac's eyes were red and streaming with

the agony of the fire he had so barely escaped through with his burden.

"Plantagenet rushed up to his granny's room," he said. "She was so high up—and now the staircase has fallen. 'Of the line of the kings,'" he repeated, his tortured eyes fixed on that attic window.

He of the "Line of the Kings," when escape was so suddenly and terribly cut off, turned, for the greatness of love's sake, a smiling face to his granny. She, often wandering, was wide adrift now in her mind.

"I think we're in the *cathadral*, Plontogo-net, love," she said, awesomely; "the can'les is a' alit."

"So they be, Granny."

"'Tis a bit of a noise about, wid the multitude, but the organ is p'alin', afar off."

"Sure 'tis a swate sound afar off from the roarin', Granny."

"Aye, it hushes ye like a mither—like a mither. I think Biddy Nolan has brought in her infant, Plontogonet; she was all'us bringin' it, wid nobody to care for it at home; 'tis a bit wailin' I heard, but 'twill soon cease.

It hushes of us all, Plontogonet, like a mither."

The armor of the Yarmouth fire department was primitive, yet the ladder reached so far that Plantagenet could save his granny.

The film was over her eyes; she clung to him in the holy trust of a great race, and he did not deny his immortal origin.

"Come now, Granny, 'tis a field o' the shamrock just outside—as ye was tellin' me about. Come, I'll lift ye over the sill. Come, till ye tread in it once more!"

He supported the frail, little, aged form, clung to it with superhuman tenacity till the strong arm of the giant below had received it; but for him to gain a footing there unaided was impossible.

"God helpin' me, I'll be back for ye, me boy!" the fireman shouted, tears streaming down the sweat and grime of his face.

Plantagenet's eyes rested with wide exultation on the deliverance of his granny; he seemed little concerned.

When the crowd below saw what he had done, and that he was biding yet a perilous chance for himself, they broke into a shout that transcended even their terror.

Plantagenet had on the cap designating him as commander of all the forces. He lifted it and smiled.

But there was no reascent of that insufficient ladder. The crash of the wall sublimely anticipated the expectation of the multitude, and the face with its halo of triumphant love sank from sight.

## CHAPTER XXI

MARGARET stood gazing as though her kinsman had lifted her into the length and breadth of some tearless knowledge, whither he had fled. When the lady was first brought out Mrs. O'Ragan had put her own shoes upon her; these stalwart coverings looked out broadly from under the richly furred dressing-gown—a relic of auspicious days. Moreover, Mrs. Shaughnessy had thrown her own ragged plaid shawl over the Stuart's head. She held it below the chin with her wasted hand, but her face was strangely heedless and young.

"Come!" said Isaac.

"And where? Where now? I have no place, except I might go with Plantagenet. But," said she, musing, unhurried, and with such unconcern as gave an air of great deliberation to her logic, " you risked your life to

save me.  Do you *wish* me to go?  I will go
where you wish."

"I have had a home for you this many a
day," said Isaac; "and it is beautiful—along
shore where you love to be.  When you are
strong we will go where you will; and Granny is waiting for you yonder in the carriage.
Come!"

Granny was telling her beads, and none
interrupted her.

"Aye, it hushes us," she murmured at the
end, "like a mither.  And so ye are goin'
to take her to the priest at last, Isik?"

"At last, mother."

"And 'tis me ye must have to the mer-
riage.  Will! will!  Plontogonet has run on
afore.  He niver was aisy like, but mus' be
all'us runnin' on afore.  Like as not he'll be
off on a bit of a progriss—the lad!  Niver
mind, 'tis in the race.  Stuart be Stuart."
She tried feebly to straighten her shrivelled
little old form.  "Stuart be Stuart.  I was
merried meself, darlin'," she said, weakly
touching Margaret, a flush of hectic joy in
her cheeks, "wid a bit of a shawl over me

head, long ago. Ah, Michael, me own loving
man, d'ye mind the tune o' the sky and the
bells that evenin'? Do ye see Plontogonet
on afore, Isik?"

Isaac bent the quiet majesty of his eyes
full upon her.

"Yes, mother," he said, "I see Plantagenet on before!"

"Thank God! It hushes us—it hushes us
all—"

With these words Granny's feet, seeking
a path from the way of tumult and bewilderment, stepped over, thus suddenly and pain-
lessly, into assured peace.

Isaac suddenly took a turn of the mind for
ostentation. Mrs. Gilchrist was *the* lady of
Yarmouth now.

Mrs. Herkimer, when invited to the sumpt-
uousness of the Stuart - Gilchrist carriage,
comported herself with an impressiveness
that would have been stultifying but for the
easy levity of Margaret's manner.

"Do you really think I used to earn seven
cents an hour, Mrs. Herkimer?"

"More, my dear Mrs. Gilchrist; far, far more!"

"Well, perhaps I did, when I drove that unspeakable beast. How *is* Eulalie? How is the colt? How is Judson?"

"Judson," said Mrs. Herkimer, "has had a useful lesson. He is quietin' down. He sees that the first gatherin' of the orchards is not always for him. The captain never used to company with him much, but I see he takes him sailin' sometimes now."

She sighed, portentously.

"I trust," she said, "that the seeds of grace in captain may be equal to this emergency."

"Oh, they will! I should feel absolutely sure!"

"You have a very happy theology, Mrs. Gilchrist," said the captain's lady, not without much sadness. "I have sometimes thought of late that Helen—"

"Well?"

"Was carryin' cheerfulness into themes where a different manner might be expected."

"Oh, Helen," said Margaret, with bright eyes and the glow of health in her cheeks—"*Helen* is my saint!"

"Mrs. Gilchrist!"

Margaret laughed encouragingly through her white teeth. "Yes, indeed, Helen is my saint. She consented to it when I was ill. Dear Mrs. Herkimer, whatever should we do without saints?"

Mrs. Herkimer did not reply, but as soon as Margaret had turned to a smiling contemplation of the landscape she put up her glasses and regarded her narrowly. "I think what she went through has touched her mind a little," she concluded. "She appears in perfect health, but she saw dreadful things. Well, perhaps He carries such!"

She sighed, replacing her spectacles in their sheath. But the Stuart understood both her act and her thought. "No, I am not '*out*'," she said, still smiling, but almost with tears in her eyes; "only, so far as any knowledge goes, I am just a wayworn, simple, superstitious Paddy! that is all!"

Mrs. O'Ragan could tell how her "own
blood - cousin, Mrs. Stuart - Gilky, ma'am,"
among other benefits, "did be takin' her for
a ride, God be thanked! so far into the
counthry as the say - wind niver smote a
feather of ye."

And indeed on this occasion the bird in
Mrs. O'Ragan's bonnet hung limp and de-
jectedly, carrying nothing in its bill forever-
more.

At which and other thoughts the blood-
cousins, Mrs. O'Ragan and Margaret, though
not always sad by any means, sometimes
wept familiarly together, as those of one
race should.

Then, one day, with a glowing sense of
graciousness, Margaret wrote to Mildred;
the substance of which letter was, in brief,
that she desired to educate and make a fine
lady of her.

But Mildred wrote back that she was too
busy, and the time was short. Aside from
other work, she had the "Army" work.
There was a girl hopelessly ill, whose comforts would be snapped short and whose

heart would be broken if she left her now.

"God bless you, dear Mrs. Gilchrist, but I cannot leave!"

Margaret hung her head. "The saints," she murmured, perplexed, "are growing on my calendar. And of how many faiths! Even Isaac—my husband—the Jew!"

But here she grew troubled again. If Margaret's brain had been touched, it was not in any point of perception; but the adamant of hereditary convictions had been broken, perhaps that flowers might spring deep where the gliding surface had been.

At present she was only conscious of disturbance. Mentally, in this respect, she was easily tired. In company, where questions were brought up which once she would have answered nonchalantly and at length in her languid, graceful voice, she blushed wearily now and avoided argument. If pressed, she had infinite ease and skill in changing the subject.

Isaac observed and smiled.

But there was one spar to which Margaret

13

clung in this sea, and as she grew to love her
husband more a great trouble concerning him
grew also in her heart.

They stood by the shore, and it was sunset
of a cool, wild day.    They had strolled on to
that little burial-place where some lay for
whom the tide had already "served."    There
was a beautiful new stone there, and it was
Isaac's gift and of Mrs. O'Ragan's selection.

"She would have those words upon it!"
said he, his whole face lighting tenderly.
" Well, she is justified!"

### PLANTAGENET STUART
### * * *
#### *Of the Line of the Kings*

A red gleam from the sky fell over the
raised marble of the letters and turned them
to gold.

" I would have added," said Isaac, the same
illumination touching his face—" I would
have added, 'On Progress '; but, though Mrs.
O'Ragan evidently disliked to thwart me,
yet she demurred at that as 'a bit playful,'
she said."

"Well, Isaac," said Margaret, whom the time now moved, "do you not think that death is solemn?—dreadful?"

"I think it is nothing," said he, the red gold from the west still shining on his face. Margaret turned to him with a slight gasp. "I think it is nothing, I know it is nothing! If we believe in God, surely we believe it is nothing. If we believe even only in nature, we *know* it is nothing—but new life! In the sense of terror and despair and finality, it has no existence except in unsound minds. See how some souls instinctively scorn it as powerless! See how Plantagenet scorned it!"

"Yes," said Margaret, "and you — you scorned it for me—I remember!"

In the impulse of this thought she almost forgot to put her next question; but now, after a little, she did so, timidly, those seeking shadows wide in her eyes—like Plantagenet's.

"And you, Isaac, do you believe in Christ?"

"With all my heart, Margaret!"

"As the Son," gasped Margaret, quickly,

in unbelieving hope, and sucking in her underlip with her own inherited sob—" as the Son
of God?"

Isaac smiled upon her perturbation.

" As the very Son of God," he said, quietly.

**THE END**

# By LILIAN BELL

FROM A GIRL'S POINT OF VIEW. 16mo, Cloth, Ornamental, Uncut Edges and Gilt Top, $1 25.

Miss Bell's former books have proved conclusively that she is a shrewd observer, and in the series of character studies which she has brought together under the title "From a Girl's Point of View " she is at her best. The book is an intimate analysis of the manner of the modern man, as seen with the eyes of the modern woman ; and it is of interest not only to those from whose stand-point it is written, but to those at whom its good-humored shafts are directed. The best of it is that Miss Bell, while she may be severe, is never unjust, and her observations are so apt that the masculine reader cannot but laugh, even while he realizes that she is dealing with one of his own short-comings.

THE UNDER SIDE OF THINGS. A Novel. With a Portrait of the Author. 16mo, Cloth, Ornamental, Uncut Edges and Gilt Top, $1 25.

Miss Bell's little story is very charming. . . . Miss Bell has plenty to say, and says it, for the most part, in a fashion engaging and simple, with touches of eloquence and passages of real strength. She has gifts of a sort far from common, and an admirable spirit. Her observation of life is keen, shrewd, and clear ; it is also sympathetic. She has a strong and easy hold on the best realities.—*N. Y. Times.*

This is a tenderly beautiful story. . . . This book is Miss Bell's best effort, and most in the line of what we hope to see her proceed in, dainty and keen and bright, and always full of the fine warmth and tenderness of splendid womanhood.—*Interior*, Chicago.

THE LOVE AFFAIRS OF AN OLD MAID. 16mo, Cloth, Ornamental, Uncut Edges and Gilt Top, $1 25.

So much sense, sentiment, and humor are not often united in a single volume.—*Observer*, N. Y.

One of the most charming books of its kind that has recently come under our notice. From its bright "Dedication" to its sweet and gracious close its spirit is wholesome, full of happy light, and one lingers over its pages.—*Independent*, N. Y.

NEW YORK AND LONDON:

HARPER & BROTHERS, PUBLISHERS

☞ *The above works are for sale by all booksellers, or will be sent by mail by the publishers, postage prepaid, on receipt of the price.*

# By MARY E. WILKINS

JEROME, A POOR MAN. A Novel. 16mo, Cloth, Ornamental, $1 50.

MADELON. A Novel. 16mo, Cloth, Ornamental, $1 25.

PEMBROKE. A Novel. Illustrated. 16mo, Cloth, Ornamental, $1 50.

JANE FIELD. A Novel. Illustrated. 16mo, Cloth, Ornamental, $1 25.

A NEW ENGLAND NUN, and Other Stories. 16mo, Cloth, Ornamental, $1 25.

A HUMBLE ROMANCE, and Other Stories. 16mo, Cloth, Ornamental, $1 25.

YOUNG LUCRETIA, and Other Stories. Illustrated. Post 8vo, Cloth, Ornamental, $1 25.

GILES CORREY, YEOMAN. A Play. Illustrated. 32mo, Cloth, Ornamental, 50 cents.

Mary E. Wilkins writes of New England country life, analyzes New England country character, with the skill and deftness of one who knows it through and through, and yet never forgets that, while realistic, she is first and last an artist.—*Boston Advertiser.*

Miss Wilkins has attained an eminent position among her literary contemporaries as one of the most careful, natural, and effective writers of brief dramatic incident. Few surpass her in expressing the homely pathos of the poor and ignorant, while the humor of her stories is quiet, pervasive, and suggestive.—*Philadelphia Press.*

It takes just such distinguished literary art as Mary E. Wilkins possesses to give an episode of New England its soul, pathos, and poetry. —*N. Y. Times.*

The pathos of New England life, its intensities of repressed feeling, its homely tragedies, and its tender humor, have never been better told than by Mary E. Wilkins.—*Boston Courier.*

The simplicity, purity, and quaintness of these stories set them apart in a niche of distinction where they have no rivals.—*Literary World,* Boston.

The charm of Miss Wilkins's stories is in her intimate acquaintance and comprehension of humble life, and the sweet human interest she feels and makes her readers partake of, in the simple, common, homely people she draws.—*Springfield Republican.*

Studies from real life which must be the result of a lifetime of patient, sympathetic observation. . . . No one has done the same kind of work so lovingly and so well.—*Christian Register*, Boston.

NEW YORK AND LONDON:

**HARPER & BROTHERS, PUBLISHERS**

☞ *The above works are for sale by all booksellers, or will be sent by the publishers, postage prepaid, on receipt of the price.*

# By MARIA LOUISE POOL

THE RED-BRIDGE NEIGHBORHOOD. A Novel. Post 8vo, Cloth, Ornamental. (*In Press.*)

IN THE FIRST PERSON. A Novel. Post 8vo, Cloth, Ornamental, $1 25.

The plot is admirable, the characters are clearly conceived and boldly drawn, and the dialogue is animated.—*Saturday Evening Gazette*, Boston.

MRS. GERALD. A Novel. Illustrated. Post 8vo, Cloth, Ornamental, $1 50.

A stirring story, a strong story, and a well-told one. The author's narrative gift is as nearly perfect as one could wish.— *Interior*, Chicago.

AGAINST HUMAN NATURE. A Novel. Post 8vo, Cloth, Ornamental, $1 25.

The contrasts of Northern and Southern temperament and manners ... are brought out with a fidelity that reveals intelligent acquaintance and trained powers of observation. This novel is far above the average.— *Watchman*, Boston.

OUT OF STEP. A Novel. Post 8vo, Cloth, Ornamental, $1 25.

THE TWO SALOMES. A Novel. Post 8vo, Cloth, Ornamental, $1 25.

KATHARINE NORTH. A Novel. Post 8vo, Cloth, Ornamental, $1 25.

MRS. KEATS BRADFORD. A Novel. Post 8vo, Cloth, Ornamental, $1 25.

ROWENY IN BOSTON. A Novel. Post 8vo, Cloth, Ornamental, $1 25.

DALLY. A Novel. Post 8vo, Cloth, Ornamental, $1 25; Paper, 50 cents.

NEW YORK AND LONDON:

## HARPER & BROTHERS, PUBLISHERS

☞ *The above works are for sale by all booksellers, or will be sent by the publishers, postage prepaid, on receipt of the price.*

www.ingramcontent.com/pod-product-compliance
Lightning Source LLC
Chambersburg PA
CBHW030341270326
41926CB00009B/921